Mega Debt-Busters.

A Christian Guide to Financial Freedom

Written and published by Joe Chiappetta
Pasadena, California, USA

www.joechiappetta.blogspot.com

TABLE OF CONTENTS

Dedication

I am so grateful for the many godly people who have shown me that, just like Jesus says in Matthew 6:24, it is impossible to serve both God and money. That truth is a daily reset button for me. I serve God, not money, thanks to Jay, Barb, Denise, Roger, Kama, Chris, Nick, Kip, Mike, and Brittany. You are the salt of the earth and have altered the course of my life for good! These chosen people serve as living examples of how to live for God while being faithful and responsible with money.

I also must thank my Mom and Dad, who spent a ton of money on taking care of our family of six. They are a great example of parents who love people while using money. All too often, the world reverses those tasks, resulting in cold individuals who love money while using people. I am very grateful that both of my parents were savvy providers who knew how to live within their financial means and keep the family out of debt.

Time and Chance and Wealth

There are a lot of books that promise financial freedom written by famous people and not so famous people. Just mentioning the phrase "financial freedom" conjures up images of people reclining at a tropical beach, in constant vacation-mode because their money is now making money for them. Theoretically, these people do not have to work; they go wherever their heart desires, and have no worries.

That is one way to look at it, and such a way *might* be a reality for a tiny minority of people. I say "might be" because I have never met anyone like that. Even people I have known with lots of money are filled with worry, strife, distraction, and especially secret sin. In fact, too many people in this position got rich often by letting the pursuit of money "own them." In other words, becoming financially free became their reason for living, often at the expense of great relationships. Consumed with greed, money becomes an idol that the greedy become devoted to above all things--even over the dear people close to them. Once such a person achieves financial freedom, that is, the freedom to not have to work, I have observed that they often still spend too much of their time worrying about how to spend and protect all that money. Material wealth therefore can become an illusion of freedom, rather than true freedom.

The thought of a rich person worrying about money when they already have lots of money might sound silly and even trivial to those not rich, but it is a huge and spiritually dangerous matter. Before you think to yourself, "If only I had such problems," think again. The inner turmoil that consumes people who have engrossed their minds to the singular thought of preserving wealth is quite draining. So many people, the rich and those aspiring to be rich, are slaves to money and the desire for money. It is a lonely lifestyle full of information overload as world financial markets and conflicting economic opinions are constantly being evaluated and analyzed--with no end in sight. I have willingly put myself under such pressures in the past, and would never want to go there again.

This is exactly why the Bible says that **"People who want to get rich fall into temptation and a trap and into many foolish and harmful desires that plunge men into ruin and destruction. For the love of money is a root of all kinds of**

evil. Some people, eager for money, have wandered from the faith and pierced themselves with many griefs." (1 Timothy 6:9-10)

What being consumed with wealth really shows is a lack of trust in God, which, in turn, brings **"many griefs"** and sucks the faith right out of a person. The trap for the wealthy and those simply aspiring to wealth is to put their emotional and physical security in their pursuit of money--as if the money can save them from everything. Therefore, whatever our financial status is, we must be very diligent to trust God as a real mental activity supported by faithful action. Trusting God is not just a religious statement. Rather, it is an immersive moment-to-moment decision. Consider carefully then, the kind of financial freedom you are seeking.

Statistically speaking, over 1 in 7 people are poor according to the Global Multidimensional Poverty Index, 2014. Most of the rest of the people are middle income, meaning that they will be working for most of the rest of their lives. These two classes, poor and middle, represent the vast majority of people, and that probably includes you and me. Do not forget that. If you do make it to riches and the promise of financial freedom, know that you are in a very elite minority. Get on your knees and thank God for it, but guard your heart so that you do not fall in love with your money, which I admit, can buy you temporary physical comfort. Then you will be in a better mindframe to know how to spend that money in a way that honors God.

1 Peter 2:16 rightly cautions us to strive for a free lifestyle and attitude while simultaneously not being irresponsible with that freedom. **"Live as free men, but do not use your freedom as a cover-up for evil; live as servants of God."** For those trying to figure out how to think about money, this means that

even when we are free, we have a duty to God. Take that duty seriously; serve God as your core style of living.

The kind of financial freedom that should be of great value to someone walking with Jesus Christ goes beyond the conventional views. Christian financial freedom is not about getting rich and living it up, doing whatever you want. Rather, it is about not letting money own you while using cash wisely and effectively to forcefully advance the divine purposes of God in our lifetime. It is not having to work so many jobs that you have no time to share your faith and study the Bible with lost people. The financial freedom I am promoting is the kind that brings worry free relationship with Christ while maximizing the amount of money that you can gain to establish wherever you live as a warm and welcoming home base of operations to advance the gospel.

To be most effective in this area, you really need to get out of debt. I am not saying that an indebted person would be ineffective in service to God. Serve God now, whether you are in debt or free from debt! But debt-free disciples of Christ, as long as they are not living to serve money, will naturally have more earnings to put into God's kingdom compared to disciples who have to split their paycheck with a line of faceless, yet persistent creditors.

Does this statement sound familiar to you? *Do well in school, get a good job, work hard, move up in your field, become wealthy, and retire in comfort as early as possible.* I can recall being a little kid at family parties and relatives, wanting to pass along practical advice to the next generation, would recite the above life plan to me, even though I was only 6 years old--as if I would remember. But I do remember because the repetition served to ingrain such a philosophy into me. In fact, many people have been hearing the school-to-wealth mantra all of their lives, because conventional thinking promotes such a pathway as the main road to financial freedom.

That is the American Dream, and it has become the whole world's dream. I have friends from China, Russia, Mongolia, and Mexico who are very vocal about how they came to the United States to grab their share of this American Dream. However, that dream is only a fragmented, elusive fantasy for most people, and that is all it will ever be for the majority. It would be so nice if the world indeed had such a simple American Dream formula of success to follow. Then people of all nations could have enough money to survive, prosper, and thrive equally. Yet that is not the case, and it has never really been the case. Moreover, as long as we are on this earth, there is much evidence to suggest that it will never be the case. Paradise is what heaven is for, not earth.

Human beings, at least the ones focused on justice for all, have on many occasions tried to imagine and even engineer the perfect world, the best economy, the most enduring civilization. But these plans continue to fall terribly short. The Bible even tells us so.

"I have seen something else under the sun: The race is not to the swift or the battle to the strong, nor does food come to the wise or wealth to the brilliant or favor to the learned; but time and chance happen to them all." - Ecclesiastes 9:11

We see from God's own word, that even the most talented and wise people will not always win. Sometimes they will lose the race, get beaten in the battle, go hungry, and go into debt. As made obvious by this passage, time and chance happen to all. So there is a "chance" that you are in debt despite making all the right decisions. You could be, as the scripture says, "brilliant," yet still the wealth does not come your way. Time and chance keep getting in your way.

For exceptionally smart and "brilliant" people who have sought, received, and followed godly advice about their finances, yet are still in debt, you might be a bit discouraged. After all, you tried to do things God's way. You have not been reckless with your money, at least not lately. So what went wrong? Perhaps nothing went wrong on your part. Maybe you made all the right moves, yet time and chance happened to you.

Perhaps you are a bit like that ancient man of faith named Job. He was hit with all sorts of tragedy: painful health problems, fortunes lost, and even children dying. Job was put through the greatest of trials as a display of faithfulness for all to see. If you read his story, you will find that Job persevered despite the terrible obstacles. He never quit on his relationship with God. In the end, God restores Job's health, gives him more children, and brings him great comfort. Eventually, Job's wealth was restored, as Job 42 confirms in verses 10 and 12. **"After Job had prayed for his friends, the Lord restored his fortunes and gave him twice as much as he had before.... The Lord blessed the latter part of Job's life more than the former part."**

With time and chance happening to all, where does God fit into this picture? Well, who do you think is the power over time and chance? God, of course. He created those concepts. In 2 Peter 3:8 it says that "**...with the Lord, a day is like a thousand years, and a thousand years are like a day.**" Therefore, God is not controlled by time. He is not stuck in the moment like we are. God controls time. In fact, time and chance are putty in the hands of God. Those in debt must face the real possibility that God may have allowed them to get into debt to teach them something. Perhaps that something is a lesson the person could never learn or fully appreciate in times of prosperity, in the comfort of all that glittering money.

I have learned so much from many previous years spent in near poverty status. Of course, I was not a willing student at the time, but such periods train a person to learn how to prioritize needs versus wants. Not many people would willingly enter such a stage of existence. We live in a world that praises luxury. But we must remember that Jesus left a life of luxury for our benefit. It was Jesus who departed from the wonder and security of paradise, became a man on this earth, and **"...made himself nothing, taking the very nature of a servant"** (Philippians 2:7).

Jesus also had **"no place to lay his head"** (Luke 9:58), which sure sounds like poverty to me. If that was not poverty, at the very least it was uncomfortability. The Bible goes into more detail about Jesus' financial status in 2 Corinthians 8:9, which states in no uncertain terms that Jesus was poor during his ministry years. **"For you know the grace of our Lord Jesus Christ, that though he was rich, yet for your sakes he became poor, so that you through his poverty might become rich."**

Before misreading the context of this verse, understand that it is about us being rich receivers of God's grace, not us gaining material wealth at the expense of Jesus. If you are a Christian, then you are modeling your life to imitate Jesus. There is really no getting around the fact that Jesus was poor on this earth. About Jesus, the Bible says that **"for your sakes he became poor."** We are called to follow him, despite all the worldly taboos that are associated with poverty. We must therefore face this sometimes uncomfortable fact: that God does discipline those he loves, and influencing what happens to our cash flow while we become misguided and/or obsessed with getting rich can certainly be part of that disciplinary process.

Hebrews 12:5-6 explains that God's discipline is not a bad thing at all, even though it might feel that way in the moment. Yet God's discipline is just the opposite: it is a sign of God's personal care and attention toward us.

"...My son, do not make light of the Lord's discipline, and do not lose heart when he rebukes you, because the Lord disciplines those he loves, and he punishes everyone he accepts as a son."

If you have made all the right financial decisions, if you have been a hard and godly worker, yet still the bills are sweeping over your head like a Hawaiian tidal wave, then feel the loving discipline of God. It hurts so good, but there must also be something powerful and vital that God wants you to learn from these troubles.

Conversely, there is also the possibility that you got into debt by way of a series of poor decisions--perhaps even sinful decisions. For example, consider the people in the days of Haggai. They **"earn wages, only to put them in a purse with holes in it."** That principle from Haggai 1:6 must be terribly frustrating to the wage earners, losing money as fast as they can make it. Why was that happening? It was a result of their neglect toward their relationship with God.

Contrasting personal homes with the house of the LORD, God calls out the people's sin in the most direct and powerful manner imaginable in Haggai 1:4. **"Is it a time for you yourselves to be living in your paneled houses, while this house remains a ruin?"** With meticulous detail, God explains that the people were focused on themselves while ignoring

God's house. Back then, that meant his temple in Jerusalem. Today it means his church, which is not a physical building, but the assembly of Jesus' faithful followers. Therefore not building up Jesus' church in favor of building up your own house is wrong. It will not end well for such a person, because it is the sin of selfishness, greed, and the pride of thinking you should honor yourself above God.

Whatever the case of how you fell into debt, by chance or by sin, the damage has been done. Now it is time to find a solution. God wants you to get on your knees and beg him for help. However you got in debt, whether by noble or ignoble means, the good news is that God is a helper. In fact, that is one of the terms used to describe the Holy Spirit in John 14:26. The Holy Spirit wants to show you how to put God first in all things, even in your closely guarded personal finances. With help from God, you could become the person God has created you to be: faithful, responsible, and able to use money to advance the holy purposes of God. Therefore, there is a way out of debt, but it takes faith and hard work.

The False god of Money

Here is the bad news; I hate to break it to you, but let us cut right to the chase. There are no shortcuts or cheat codes to getting out of debt. Gambling and get-rich-quick schemes are not part of this guide. Becoming debt-free takes hard work and sacrifice. First however, you must retrain your mind by embracing financial and biblical concepts that may seem radical on our consumer comfort oriented planet.

We live in a society that holds to one core value: "show me the money, and if you cannot, you will be denied privileges and suffer." No one may come right out and say this, but that is how it is. If you do not believe me, try waiting until your family is hungry, leave your wallet at home, take your family to a restaurant, and ask the staff there if they would feed your nice family even though you did not bring any money.

Yes, the world revolves around money because it has become more than a tool to exchange value; money has become an idol to so many. That means money is a false god, and people will suffer to get close to this false god. In fact, people will suffer hourly to get more and more money. Yet people hate to suffer, so they try to make up all kinds of ways to cheat the system; I have tried it too, with no net gain--only loss. The world is full of futile attempts to delay payment as long as possible. In most cases, what this really is involves putting off the pain of paying for a later time period. Most of these ways involve getting into various degrees of debt, as if debt will make the suffering go away. Yet in most cases, debt does the exact opposite. Debt increases, as does confusion, despair, more debt, and more suffering.

"Those who run after other gods will suffer more and more...." - Psalm 16:4

See the paradox here. The more you chase after money and idolize it, the more your sorrows increase. Regardless of whether you actually find more money, you do not get happier running after the false god of money. You get sad and suffer. An ironic characteristic of these situations is that we create the problem. This is best shown in Jeremiah 16:20. **"Do men make their own gods? Yes, but they are not gods!"** Turning money into a false god is an ancient practice people have been perfecting for centuries. It is no wonder that the pain associated with this false god gets greater and greater.

The only way out of this pit of suffering is to attack the very behavior that got you into debt. But first you have to see it. That means you need to change how you think and how you run--how you operate. Have you been running after another god? And is the name of that other god "Money"?

The Fog of Materialistic Confusion

Is having debt bad? Is it possible to bust out of debt? Here is a sentence you never want anyone to say to you; "You owe us lots of money. Now we own you!" Fully stated or implied yet unsaid, this is a harsh reality that a growing number of people are falling into. People are in financial debt, and enslaved in the process. When you are in that situation it really does feel like other people own you, because you are basically living to pay them off. Most of your time goes to working so that your debtors (owners) stay happy with you remaining enslaved to the chains of paying them interest on the debt. That is their source of income. The debtor lives and prospers off of you--like a leach.

If that disturbs you, it should. We have good reason to be very careful about abusing money. The Russian author Leo Tolstoy wrote about this passionately in the early 1900s. In his book *What Shall We Do?*, Tolstoy said "Money is a new form of slavery differing from the old form of slavery only by its impersonality, by the freedom it gives from all human relations to the slave."

While not the direct subject of this book, philosophers, economists, and even former world leaders have written quite clearly about the dangers of our financial system. After digesting what I can, I am left with a strong and unsettling impression that most things having to do with money (generosity aside), are a deadly trap for all kinds of pitfalls and evil schemes. Therefore tread carefully in your spending of money.

As you talk to more and more people, you might think that, "everybody is doing it... everyone is in some kind of debt." Whether you have a car loan, home mortgage, student loans, the dreaded maxed-out credit cards, or overdue bills, debt is debt and it can take you down for the count if you are not careful. Just because everyone might be in some sort of debt, does that make it right? Of course not.

I remember being a teenager when I first started to understand how financially complicated and restrictive the world had become. Everything was expensive and no one seemed to like the system--not even the people running that system. But the adults seemed to put up with our messed up economy without a fight. Why would any reasonable person tolerate such inequity?

There developed a strong desire in me to rebel against this system that I did not approve of. My alarm went something like this; "You mean to tell me that for me to make my creative paintings and write books, and expect to make a decent living from those endeavors, it would be only a long shot, at best? That really stinks!" I became angry over this world I did not create. Little did I know that my real battle was with God the creator, who allowed the world to get in such a state. I failed to see how this was part of God's plan to humble and refine me into a person of character and integrity. I am still working on that.

It took me years to accept the fact that to survive, most people, including me, would work at jobs that they would hardly care about, if not for the money. That was the real world? I wanted no part of it.

Therefore, I vowed at that idealistic young age to never get sucked into the materialistic net that was tightening over the whole world, and enslaving so many to jobs that they hated. I learned to do without things, not so much because I love to suffer, but more so because I could not stand the concept that somewhere, someone was waiting to catch me being careless and enslave me into debt. I was resolved to never let that happen.

It is almost thirty years later. How am I doing with that resolve? Not amazing, but not too bad either. Over the years, I've still had more than a few jobs that I did not like. But in the fight against materialism, my wife and I are doing pretty good. Our only debt was a home mortgage, which was paid off a few years ago.

However, I know how easy it is to get pulled into the fog of materialistic confusion. I currently own a desktop computer and a laptop computer. Both of them run way slower than the latest models, and in view of the current advertising campaigns, they seemed a bit old and outdated.

Therefore, I got it in my head that I needed a new computer, even though I bought the desktop computer only one year ago. A trip to the big electronics store and $800 later, I found myself looking at the unopened box of the super-fast laptop that I had just purchased. Owning such a thing of power made me very happy--too happy.

A nagging question suddenly entered my brain; "Do I really NEED this computer?" Have I been bowing down to the false god of materialism? The question kept running in my mind for the next few days, and influenced me not to even open the box! Finally, ten agonizing days later, I returned that computer for a full refund. I did not need it after all. The proof was in the fact that most of the ten books that I had written and published in the past decade were all produced with computers that I already owned. That is not bad for an "old and outdated" device.

Encounters such as mine should help remind us that there are many Bible verses that caution against people trying take on things they do not need, or trying to do too much at once. King Solomon, famous for being the wisest man of his era, said **"Better one handful with tranquillity than two handfuls with toil and chasing after the wind"** (Ecclesiastes 4:6). There is much to be said about the peace and quiet of a simple life, free from materialism. The king gave this advice because people have a greedy nature to grab after stuff they do not really need. God wants us free of the complexities and uncertainties that come with debt.

So what happened to the $800 refund? Putting it into new technology that would soon be as outdated as my current computers was a waste. That is chasing after the wind. Gambling it into the stock market seemed just as unstable and possibly futile--at least for me--because I did not have the time to read up on all the company dynamics it takes to pick a winner.

I am not saying people cannot play the stock market. Some make money at it, but (and this is a big one) some lose money at it--a lot of money. It is not a sure thing, so get lots of advice from people who know your whole situation. For my family, making a double payment on our home mortgage... that would save us money on interest payments for certain, and godly people advised us how to make that happen. That is what we do on the road to being debt-free.

A disclaimer needs to be added here regarding double payments (or extra payments) toward a mortgage. Yes, this is a good long-term money-saving plan, but only if you can afford to do this while still also being generous toward God. However, if you are making double mortgage payments while also not being generous toward God, the Bible warning about reaping what you sow (Galatians 6:7) must be considered. In other words, you will get out of a relationship precisely what you put in. Therefore, for the person who does not financially give to God in faith, what will grow out of that is... no faith!

Conversely, for the person who financially gives to God consistently in faith, that person will also reap (gather, collect) more faith, and even material blessings. I have seen this in my own life, and in the lives of the faithful friends who have taught me the godly principles of giving generously. It can also be confirmed in numerous places in the Bible. Most directly, in 2 Corinthians 9:6, Paul writes **"Remember this: Whoever sows sparingly will also reap sparingly, and whoever sows generously will also reap generously."** Therefore look at God as the ultimate giver who extends the reach and the rewards for the little givers (us) who strive to imitate him.

The ultimate goal is to be wise and generous with what God has given you. If you do invest in something in which you expect a financial return on investment (ROI), in addition to getting lots of advice from godly people first, make sure that your ROI comes in at a higher percentage than the interest rate of your debt. If it does not, then it is certainly better to pay off the debt quicker and not to invest in things that get you a lower financial return. For example, if the interest rate on your debt is 4%, then you would not buy a stock that is only projected to increase by 3%. In this scenario, you would not invest your money in any financial deals unless the ROI is more than 4% by the most conservative estimates.

As another cautionary guideline, if you have a history of impulsive gambling losses, then it would be best to simply stay away from the stock market or similar venues altogether. Remember that we want one handful of peace rather than two handfuls of toil and chasing after the wind.

So we can sum up by reminding ourselves to be urgent, calculated, and wise about getting out of debt. Yet in the process, we must not neglect God and his kingdom.

Money Gathered Little by Little

As most people who have read the Bible even a little bit know well, the main focus of the book is not to guide the reader toward fast economic growth. However, when the Bible does address personal financial growth, take special note of it. Consider it the most golden tip from on high. One of the Bible's most direct statements about how to expand the amount of money you have comes in Proverbs 13:11.

Dishonest money dwindles away, but he who gathers money little by little makes it grow."

There you have it: personal financial advice from the Almighty God on how to grow your net worth. From time to time, we all dream of finding a big windfall of cash, but God advises **"little by little"** financial growth. This is on the humbling side: say goodbye to that overnight rags-to-riches fantasy. Gathering money is effective when it is gathered in small but steady increments.

Do you have the patience for slow, yet incremental monetary growth? Redo your budget, seek and find the higher paying job that positions you to earn more than you spend, and save a little every month. That is where you need to start.

The latter part of this proverb is actually the part that most people miss. They gather money, but they do not make it grow because they put the money in places where it will be spent. The key is to gather the money over time and place it where it cannot be spent up so easily. Don't put it in a checking account; that will be gone by the end of the month. Place a portion of this little-by-little money where it will be very difficult for you to spend. Save some and invest some if you can afford to take such a risk.

We all want a solid return on our investments. I have done very well with real estate, but that doesn't mean you will. Markets fluctuate. I know others who have done well with stocks that pay steady dividends, but these folks have been in it for over four decades.

Yet again, time and chance happen to all. A good stock one year could be terrible the next. What I am saying is really this: beyond the kingdom of God, world evangelism, and giving to the poor, I have no idea what else you should invest any additional portion of your money in. But it would be prudent for you to educate yourself over time about where you think the growth might come from. Pray about it. Test the waters, get more advice, and perhaps invest a little in that. But there are no guarantees when it comes to investments in this world.

In fact, no human being really knows where the next big thing to invest in will be. The economy is salted with so much uncertainty. Most financial advisors will give you an investment plan to increase your earnings, and they will tell you to diversify your investments because of market uncertainties. To further protect themselves, these financial investment professionals typically qualify their advice with a disclaimer statement somewhere in their fine print. Summed up, such disclaimers basically say that the financial adviser could be totally wrong, and you could lose money instead of gaining money.

Moreover, I would say the same thing if I were telling someone about one particular investment, or another one. We don't know the future, so we can only make somewhat educated guesses about what might happen next. The scriptures even remind us of such things in Ecclesiastes 8:7. **"Since no man knows the future, who can tell him what is to come?"** Think about this verse the next time some expert assures you where to invest your money because of their supposed insight into the future. The financial markets could grow, stagnate, decline, or even crash based on so many unknown factors. In a global economy, it is impossible to predict with certainty from one day to the next because the variables are literally worldwide.

In his wisdom, God has us cut out all the guesswork, because in many cases, we do not even know our right hand from our left hand (Jonah 4:11). The Lord makes it clear: gathering money "little by little" is the way to go. Don't spend it all on meeting your needs. That is how you make it grow. This takes frugality, denying materialistic desires, long term hard work, and patience. Getting out of debt, therefore, will come "little by little." Take a deep breath. Muster up all the patience that you have and dig deep to find more. That is what it will take to get out of debt. Little by little, as you grow in wisdom, discipline, and patience, you will see your debt being reduced until finally, after consistent financial repositioning, you will become a mega debt-buster too.

Greed in the Bible

Some think greed is a good quality because it preserves and protects self-interest so a person can prosper. This is so wrong. Greed is like a little unnoticed worm that slowly coils around you and stretches until you are completely under its control. Then you are stuck in slavery to serve the greedy desires that have taken hold of your otherwise fine senses. It has happened to me multiple times over the years. Each time I give in to greed, it is more embarrassing and humiliating than the previous time. I should know better--learn from experience. But when I let my guard down and get even just a little greedy, that evil worm expands to make matters worse every time.

Let us take a deeper look into what the Bible says about what our heart towards money should be. In the Parable of the Sower, notice in Mark 4:19 that the third soil is the person who gets choked out by **"the deceitfulness of wealth."** This means that a person can literally be tricked in their thinking when possessing or pursuing wealth. Jesus is saying that the very nature of financial wealth has a deceiving quality to it. In other words, money can mess with your brain.

Luke 12:13-15 shows that there are all kinds of greed--as if we are surrounded by greed. Jesus clearly speaks against it. **"...Watch out! Be on your guard against all kinds of greed. Life does not consist in an abundance of possessions."**

How much are money and possessions attached to your heart? Are you on the lookout for any hooks of greediness that may have snuck into your personality? If Jesus says to **"Watch out,"** then that is exactly what we need to do. Look more carefully; there are **"all kinds of greed,"** and none of them are good for you. In other words, there are so many variations of greed, that unless you are seriously alert and consistently on your guard, you might not recognize all the greed in your own behavior. As an individual, and as a whole nation, people's hearts can become corrupt through greedy desires.

If you study Ezekiel 28:1-9, an ancient yet still relevant path to greed is exposed. Because of wealth, many hearts grow proud, as in possessing an elevated sense of importance and arrogance. People develop false ideas as if they are their own gods. It is a dangerous path to go down. Greed promotes pride and self-idolatry. And pride promotes the illusion that we do not need God. It is a slippery slope. Turning back to God in humility stops the sliding into oblivion. Yet if a person stays in a state of greed and pride, they have the nerve to compete with God, as if their own power can make them great. We must remember that we do not create ourselves. God is the creator. **"He brings one down, he exalts another."** (Psalm 75:7)

When thinking more about pride, how it can give a person an elevated sense of importance, do we really want to compete with God? I have been foolish enough to try to compete with, and even play god on too many occasions in my past. Not surprisingly, I lost miserably every time. So have you. Therefore let God be exalted (lifted up) in your life while you humble yourself (lower yourself) in submission to his will.

1 Timothy 6:6-10 is such a powerful passage to expose and oppose greed, that I believe some people with great faith and self-discipline can simply read it and repent immediately of greed. In verse 10 is the famous phrase about how **"...the love of money is the root of all kinds of evil."**

This alone is a true statement that the greedy would do well to memorize and dwell on daily. Think about it; Loving money--not just possessing money--leads to all kinds of evil! That means poor, indebted people can create all kinds of evil by their adoration and aspirations (love) for money. A person can be a severely low income individual with only the money he received from begging in his pocket, yet he may still love and adore the concept of having money--just the idea of it. Make no mistake; this is not just a rich-people passage. This warning is for us all.

Let's look at the whole passage of 1 Timothy 6:6-11. **"But godliness with contentment is great gain. For we brought nothing into the world, and we can take nothing out of it. But if we have food and clothing, we will be content with that. Those who want to get rich fall into temptation and a trap and into many foolish and harmful desires that plunge people into ruin and destruction. For the love of money is a root of all kinds of evil. Some people, eager for money, have wandered from the faith and pierced themselves with many griefs. But you, man of God, flee from all this, and pursue righteousness, godliness, faith, love, endurance and gentleness."**

See how an eagerness for money leads people to wander away from their faith, ending up **"with many griefs"**? People who once had faith literally fall away from God simply over getting too excited and aggressive about finances. When you are in debt, understand that there is a great temptation to pour all of your heart and strength into getting out of debt, like a captive animal tearing at a hunter's net thrown over it. Yet such frantic focus on financial matters can turn into another way of expressing a love for money. I am not saying that you should not strive to get out of debt, but do not let this goal consume you. Remember that we cannot take our money or our debt status with us to the grave.

Therefore, we must find contentment in our relationship with God. That is where the "great gain" is: **"godliness with contentment is great gain."** Are you content--no matter what? Are you satisfied with the life God has given you? If there is a good deal of discontent (unsettled) notions in your heart, ask yourself how many of those items of discontent have to do with money.

The desire for riches is an instant crash landing. As stated in 1 Timothy 6:6-11, it brings a person to **"fall into temptation and a trap."** It's also full of **"foolish and harmful desires"** that lead to **"ruin and destruction."** How much more direct do we need it to be? See how easily the desire for money can cloud people's judgment and lead many astray? This is dangerous stuff. As the Bible says, **"flee from all this,"** as in, run away from any urge or scheme that places money *or even the idea of money* close to your heart.

God does not call people to material wealth; he calls people to love one another. Are you here to rescue people, or feed your own greed? Remember that God can do amazing things with our money and our faith when we trust him and not money.

A great scripture that demonstrates this is in Psalm 17:14. **"O LORD... You still the hunger of those you cherish; their sons have plenty, and they store up wealth for their children."** What does God do for those he cherishes? He takes care of their hunger; he provides. Notice that it does not say that the person will never experience hunger. Rather when there is hunger, God will **"still"** it. So God is looking for people who trust him through times of hunger. Then the whole family prospers, then the **"sons have plenty."**

Yet this all goes back to being cherished in the sight of God. Does God cherish you? Are you seeking a life that pleases him? God will not cherish the greedy. Those who love money cannot love God (Matthew 6:24). Do not put your hope in wealth, but in God. Learn your lesson; greed is NOT good. It is a killer.

Greed Is One Click Away

Lately I have become more aware of God's hand in my everyday life. He has been using challenging situations to train me in so many areas. Specifically, God has been exposing my pride, limits to my love, and greed. The more I see it, the more appalled that I am; how unlike the Lord am I? So very much!

Nevertheless, I am convinced that the more I do see of my sin, the more I desire to change and be like Jesus! I will make every effort to operate in a state of repentance, no matter how far I fall short. When knocked down, I simply need to keep getting back up. It reminds me of this verse from Psalm 75:6-7. **"No one from the east or the west or from the desert can exhaust a man. But it is God who judges: He brings one down, he exalts another."**

We see that God is a maker and a breaker. Do not take all the credit when things go well for you; know that God has exalted you. Conversely, if things are not going well, know that God may be bringing you down to teach you something vital. This is about trusting God in all things. If we are in financial decline or prosperity, look to God with humility either way. Our lives are in his hands. He is intricately involved in our endeavors, as also is evident in Proverbs 17:3. **"The crucible for silver and the furnace for gold, but the LORD tests the heart."**

I see God refining, judging, testing, lifting up, and bringing down in my life. Trusting him is the lesson regardless of circumstances. I do trust him at this moment. The challenge is to maintain that trust on a moment-to-moment level. I hope that you will do so as well. After many long years, I understand that God brings down and lifts up people on a spiritual as well as physical level. It is his refining process.

This refining is evident in many areas of my life, including my career. I have worked for a long time in the challenging field of helping people with disabilities get jobs. Multiple times each year, I wonder if I should switch to a different field. But this is where God has put me for most of my years as a follower of Jesus. I have been doing this for over 16 years: some years better than others. I have seen so much: heartache, neglect, pain, poverty, victory, foolishness, empowerment, and greed. Truly there is nothing new under the sun. Despite the hardship of this job, I do thank God for all that he has taught me in this long journey.

The disability employment industry has gone through some very serious funding cuts lately and it has affected me in many ways: some of which are more disturbing than others. Recent events have even led me into a very serious battle with my own greed!

It all started when I had to take a job that was $25,000 lower than my previous position which had ended due to funding cuts. That was a huge financial hit. Therefore I felt a mounting pressure to figure out how to make more money. I was applying for other jobs, but not getting any job offers. Therefore I started researching other ways to make money and came across an online website that basically pays the user in tiny amounts of digital currency just for going to their site and letting a video game advertisement play for about 30 seconds. Each visit is equivalent to earning only a small fraction of a penny.

Now mind you, I am usually a fairly reasonable person. Yet I am alarmed at how quickly all rationality went out of my mind. I started using that site and found a few other sites like it: thinking that if I can find enough sites which pay for clicking, then those fractions of money will soon turn into big earnings. That is easy money for a little brainless work. Perhaps I can even teach unemployed people with disabilities to do this and they can make money at it too.

What I did not realize is that such brainless activity soon captured what was left of my intellect and made me less focused. I degraded into a greedy fool, ever obsessed with getting just a little more. As the old Glenn Frey song, *Smuggler's Blues* goes, "The lure of easy money, it has a very strong appeal."

This practice escalated for a few weeks until I had a public come-to-Jesus moment. At church during the sermon, while sitting in the front row I was taking notes on my smartphone about the sermon. I have been doing that for years and it works great for searching old lessons and topics that I quickly want to revisit.

Yet this day, right in the middle of the sermon, I got a notification on my phone that one of the ad sites was ready for me to visit it so that I could click on my reward. Despite the fact that I knew this was wrong--clicking on such things at church--and that the sermon was even about greed, I did not resist. I turned down the brightness on my phone so as not to draw too much attention to myself, and then I clicked on that notification.

Now that is not the worst of it. Usually, what happens at this point is that a video game ad pops up and plays automatically, yet I ignore it for about 30 seconds by putting the phone in my pocket. Then, once the ad has finished playing, I make two more clicks and then I get the pennies or fractions of pennies (it varies). The ad is easy to ignore with the sound off. It is not very intrusive since it is merely running in the darkness of my pocket. As for mental energy, it adds up to only a few seconds of distraction--five at the most. What harm can come of that?

I soon found out. This day, sitting quietly in the front row and center row of church, during the sermon, after clicking on the site, the ad plays as usual, but much to my surprise, the sound is on--at full volume! But even that is not the worst of it. It is not the sound of a catchy jingle that could be mistaken for a phone ringtone. What everyone around me hears is the alarming, interruptive, and adrenaline-pumping sound of battle and gunfire--all emanating from me and my "smart" phone.

I instantly go into shock and cover-up mode. Yet the brains went completely out of me. I tried to stop or pause the ad from continuing, but the screen would not respond. The unmistakable noise of bullets boomed throughout the congregation. The greed that had hovered one click away had now taken center stage in my life, and in the house of God.

Gratefully, my wife, sitting next to me, quickly grabbed the phone, found the volume button, and turned it down to silent. The crisis was over. I recall being most impressed with the fact that my wife could do all that while still having the mental capacity to lean into me and whisper "Joseph?!?" in indignant disapproval.

The whole disruption lasted only about three seconds, but the incident cut my heart three miles long. An embarrassing fog had lifted from my eyes. I realized how foolish, deceitful, and greedy I had become. I was disrespectful to the preacher, who is also my friend, I was disrespectful to the church, and most importantly, I was disrespectful to God, who allowed me to have the funds to even buy and maintain such a nice smartphone.

The next 24 hours were spent praying, apologizing, confessing my sin, and of course, removing the app that was cleverly designed to tantalize all my greedy desires. Repentance is refreshing and I am glad to be free of this disgusting behavior. I remain humbled, or should I say humiliated, that after almost two decades of walking as a follower of Jesus, I could still so easily and quickly fall into such a dark, dishonorable, and greedy way of operating. Thanks be to God for his grace, patience, and direction not to love money.

All the warnings about greed in the Bible have now become magnified--they make so much more sense. One of the most straightforward verses about greed is 1 Timothy 6:17. **"Command those who are rich in this present world not to be arrogant nor to put their hope in wealth, which is so uncertain, but to put their hope in God, who richly provides us with everything for our enjoyment."**

Especially in light of my recent epic exposure of greed, we need to keep this command on our hearts. We can learn here that wealth is **"so uncertain."** This uncertainty, by the way, can also be easily seen in the ups and downs of the stock market. The only acceptable behavior, even for those currently rich, is to put their hope in God. It takes trust to believe that God is a rich provider, because so much happens, not on our timetable, but on God's timetable.

Test yourself in this direction. The Bible commands you not to put your hope in wealth because it is grossly uncertain. Before you dismiss this because you do not perceive yourself as a rich person, understand that if you have food in your refrigerator and any money in the bank, then you are richer than most people in the world. In that light, ask yourself where your hope is planted. Does your security come from money? Then you have a problem with God.

If you do put your hope in money, then there is also a pretty high probability that you have such a strong desire to spend money, that you have likely used it too much on things that you cannot afford. Consequently now, that is why you are in debt. You are not willing to suffer the discomfort of going without things that you simply could not afford.

Most people in debt need to see that the root of debt is greed. I'm sure there are some exceptions, like those who have sudden and urgent medical procedures that are outrageously priced and such things lead them into unexpected debt. Yet for most people that is not the case. We get into debt because we buy things that we think are needs but they are really not needs; they are merely strong desires and the purchase is made to appease our insecurities.

Therefore we must understand that greed is not our friend. Are you alarmed about your own greed? I hope my encounter with greed will leave you with a sense of awe and holy fear of God. Standing in opposition to greed is God himself. You cannot win against God, and the greedy cannot stand against God. Greed is not good--not one bit of it. Greed is our enemy. Greed will destroy us if we do not repent of it. As I have discovered the hard way, beware! Greed is only one click away.

The Pride of Money

We think we are so smart sometimes. I know I am not the only one guilty of this thought. We know greed is bad; we have heard all the warnings against greed. So we will watch out for greed while we still go about our very own way, wheeling and dealing, and then coming out on top financially... because we are so very intelligent. But are we really that smart? Proverbs 16:25 will put us in our place--every time. **"There is a way that seems right to a man, but in the end it leads to death."**

In the context of money spending, it is so often that we are deeply convinced that we know how best to spend money. Our way seems so right, like we are the elite experts who know the future, or at least know our own future, which is simply ridiculous. Only God knows the future.

Young's Literal Translation captures the drama and tragedy infused into this same verse from Proverbs; **"There is a way right before a man, And its latter end--ways of death."**

I can vividly picture a wise elderly person, dressed in a faded, tattered robe, firmly whispering this passage in my ear as a passionate warning, and at the end leaning in closer, eyes widened, glancing about, and then peering firmly into my soul while emphasizing that last phrase in a scratchy, low voice: "ways of death!"

What is pride? It is thinking you know better, operating with an elevated sense of self-importance. Pride makes you certain that what you are doing (your way) is right because you are you. But that does not make your ways any more right. Pride typically makes your ways wrong, dead wrong. When pride and money mingle--even just a little money--it is such a toxic combination: watch out.

Think of the ambitious art student embracing $100,000 in college loans while ignoring the fact that only 1 in 10 art school graduates actually work in the art field after graduation. That is pride.

How about the long term unemployed person who passes up certain jobs because they are "beneath him," or not in the proper field of interest. That is pride too. The list goes on. To grow, we must embrace the often ignored, yet excellent advice: swallow your pride!

Not long ago I had to do that very thing. My high paying job ended and I was offered a new position at a new company without even filling out any job application. There was just one small problem. If I took this job, it would be a $25,000 pay cut from my previous job. I wrestled with the thought of going "backwards" on the income earning scale. Don't they know what I'm worth? (Can you see the pride cropping up?)

As I deliberated, I sought more advice from people of faith. They reminded me that some money is better than no money. Therefore, I "lowered" myself and came to my senses: any job is better than no job. So I took that job, added amazing new experiences and accomplishments to my resume, and less than a year later, it led to another new job making the same as my old high paying position. That is a happy ending, but if I had not swallowed my pride, I might still be unemployed. The pride of pursuing more money almost elevated me to being a fool and missing out on the present opportunity.

Pride leading to foolishness is a theme in the Bible. Consider Job 21:14-15. Referring to the wicked, Job shows how foolish pride can be; **"Yet they say to God, 'Leave us alone! We**

have no desire to know your ways. Who is the Almighty, that we should serve him? What would we gain by praying to him?'"

Job understood, as we need to understand, that pride makes us think we do not need God. What a foolish thought! We become deceived that life is good on our own power, with our own money that we made with our own two hands and our own hard work.

Such thinking, of course, is opposed to the holy calling to trust in God, not self. As alluded to in the beginning of that passage from Job, pride leaves the foolish "alone," giving up on prayer and therefore giving up on relationship with God. Imagine again, the wise old person leaning in to hit home the closing argument: "Beware the pride of money. Its latter end--ways of death!"

Debt in the Bible

As much as we sometimes wish it were some other way, we see that God has put us in a world where we have to make money and spend money to survive. Yet we must not become greedy or prideful about it. This is a lifelong test of our hearts. So we need direction about how to use this powerful little thing called money without getting consumed by it. Gratefully, we do not have to wing it when it comes to spending money and understanding debt. The Bible is full of rock-solid financial advice and direction. Let's investigate what the New Testament has to say about debt, as Jesus tells the parable of the unmerciful servant.

"Therefore, the kingdom of heaven is like a king who wanted to settle accounts with his servants. As he began the settlement, a man who owed him ten thousand talents was brought to him. Since he was not able to pay, the master ordered that he and his wife and his children and all that he had be sold to repay the debt. The servant fell on his knees before him. 'Be patient with me,' he begged, 'and I will pay back everything.' The servant's master took pity on him, canceled the debt and let him go."
- Matthew 18:23-27

- Being in debt puts you and your whole family at risk!

- God is forgiving. He is willing to cancel debt.

- But are people in the world forgiving about debt like God is? No. My own experience, as well as the scriptures, confirm this.

"But when that servant went out, he found one of his fellow servants who owed him a hundred denarii. He grabbed him and began to choke him. 'Pay back what you owe me!' he demanded. His fellow servant fell to his knees and begged him, 'Be patient with me, and I will pay you back.' But he refused. Instead, he went off and had the man thrown into prison until he could pay the debt."
- Matthew 18:28-30

- Too often, forgiven people do not remember what they themselves have been forgiven from. Consequently, they fail to pass along that forgiveness.

- The business world is typically unforgiving and cold-hearted about debt. Companies go through tremendous efforts to get you to buy their products and pretend to care about you. That is what marketing campaigns are for. Yet when you cannot make your payments, that same "caring" company may hound you and forcefully take possession of whatever they can get out of you. They will throw every law in the book at you to get as much money as they can out of you, regardless of how it ruins your life. Think about the very nature of a for-profit company. It exists to start with a little money and make much more money. If you interact with that company at all, you can be certain that the for-profit company has a plan to get profits from you. For-profit companies, no matter what they say and promote, care about your money, not you.

- By contrast, God cares about you, not your money. Forgiving debt is more important to God than increasing profits.

- God has a better perspective about money. His view is pure and humane. Trust his view.

- Debt can deposit you into a world of trouble and even rob your freedom. I wonder how many headaches out there are caused by the stress that comes with debt. This, of course, leads to more expenses: headache medicines, anti-anxiety medication, and so on.

- Harsh creditors and harsh treatment can come to those in debt.

- If the unmerciful servant was in his right mind, he would not have been cruel to his fellow man. The pressure of being in debt often makes people do things that are shameful.

- Expect to be mistreated when you are in debt. It is nothing new. Do not waste time feeling sorry for yourself. Rather, become urgent and aggressive about getting out of debt in a godly manner.

- Take an inventory of all the things you bought over the years that are now underused, decaying, and just taking up space. Sell what you can (probably at a loss), but wouldn't you rather have done without that stuff in the first place and put the money toward your debt? It is too late now, but learn from it. Materialism must die!

Close Encounters of the Materialistic Kind

You might think that I learned my lesson about materialism from the $800 returned computer incident. Almost! If you are anything like me, then it might take a few times of repeated lessons before a concept truly sinks in and becomes who you are. There are a few terms for this behavior, and none of them are good: pride, stubborn, forgetful, dull... you get the picture.

Becoming aware of stubbornness is an important step in changing a person's spending patterns. Unfortunately, I almost repeated the pattern with another geek gadget that I did not really need.

Here is an additional example of how the desire for things can blind a person to the simplicity of reason. A little while before I bought that $800 laptop, I found out that a new smartphone with the largest screen available ever was finally on sale in

America. I had been following the development of this phone for the previous 16 months in the news. Now I could actually buy one. For only $400, I could be the owner of the best smartphone on the planet. Plus, the device came preloaded with two hit movies: Transformers I and Transformers II. How could any man-geek resist?

I went to the phone's exclusive US dealer on the afternoon of the day it was released, but it was sold out--not just in that store, but nationwide! Sad-faced on the way home, another influential thought entered my mind; "I already have a big smartphone and it works just fine. Plus, I already saw the first Transformers movie, and I heard that the second movie was not as good."

It was as if a new and foreign concept had entered my realm of consciousness. As stated previously, the materialistic fog had been lifted away. To this day, I am content with my 4 year old, yet quite reliable phone. It has the second biggest screen on the planet. Nothing too shabby. Yet I had a list for more and more--how very foolish of me.

In addition to overcoming that round of materialism, I realized something quite useful about my almost-purchased phone. If we had $400 to almost spend on a phone, then we naturally had $400 to actually pay down toward the house payment. And that is what we did. Does it come as a surprise to anyone that we paid off that house in record time?

Geek gadget matters aside, urgency is what my wife and I have practiced for years regarding financial matters. When we bought our home, during the beginning years of paying off our mortgage, one number appalled me every month; We were paying way more on interest than we were on the value of the home. If this pattern kept up, we'd be enslaved to the mortgage company for the next thirty years. **"The rich get**

richer, the poor get the picture!" as the hopeless and disgruntled Midnight Oil song goes.

That sense of alarm about what a rip off it would be for the bank to get all that interest money from us was a big motivator. No one from the bank had ever even been to my home. All I was to the bank was an easy income stream. I was easy money to them.

Such hard realities forced my wife and I to create a budget, stick to it, and cut back drastically on all areas of our spending. This has been a sacrifice, but well worth it. As mentioned earlier, we stayed on target to pay off that house in twelve years instead of thirty. Later we sold that property at a considerable profit. We could not have done any of that without consistent application of the spiritual principles covered in this book. I thank God for lifting me out of the fog of materialistic confusion.

Go Old Testament on Your Debt

The following Old Testament law might shock you, but it is important to look at the things that God himself put in place to keep us out of the slavery that comes with debt.

"At the end of every seven years you must cancel debts. This is how it is to be done: Every creditor shall cancel the loan he has made to his fellow Israelite. He shall not require payment from his fellow Israelite or brother, because the LORD's time for canceling debts has been proclaimed. You may require payment from a foreigner, but you must cancel any debt your brother owes you." - Deuteronomy 15:1-3

- God set up rules to protect his people from long term debt.

- Do not go by your own rules. You cannot possibly come up with better rules than God. His rules are in place to shield you.

- He knows that long term debt can leave you without a shield and sorely unprotected.

- This verse is also more proof that the Bible is from God and not man. When has any human government ever created such kind and forgiving laws for the people? Only a true creator (God) would think on such a merciful level to put such a refreshing principle into law.

"For the LORD your God will bless you as he has promised, and you will lend to many nations but will borrow from none. You will rule over many nations but none will rule over you." - Deuteronomy 15:6

Do not be misled and think that this verse applies to the glory days of the United States of America, which was somewhat founded on a number of Christian principles. As it is operating today, the USA is not a nation walking in obedience to God. Therefore, the promises and blessings of God are not simply going to be blanketed over every citizen. That means what each person does individually is of the utmost importance. So, in terms of financial insight, what can we get out of this verse?

- God does not want his people borrowing from the world (in debt). If you consider yourself a person of God, avoid borrowing, or only do so as a very last resort. Why?

- When this principle is ignored, many nations (or corporations) will rule over you. Moreover, your family is at risk. This was true even in ancient times, as reflected in the book of Job, which took place about 1700 BC.

"...the infant of the poor is seized for a debt." - Job 24:9

- Debt can lead to slavery, no matter what era you live in.

- Today though, we just do not call it slavery, because that is politically incorrect. Yet, how many workers slave away at two jobs while their kids are placed in before-school care, a full school day, and then after-school care? At the end of the day, parents have nothing, or next to nothing left to give emotionally to their children. I know. I have been there, and it is not pretty.

Some may try to rationalize debt by crying out, "But you do not understand! Times are hard and we need to borrow to survive." It may be true that times are hard, but operating in a prolonged state of debt is simply not righteous--even in hard times. Take the book of Ezekiel, for instance. It was written around 600 BC while Ezekiel and his entire nation were captive in a foreign land. You might think that in such extreme conditions, taking on a little debt here and there might seem reasonable: after all, how much opportunity can a person have while being held in a strange land against their will? Yet a closer look at Ezekiel 18 has an eye-opening list of righteous behaviors, written precisely while the people were in captivity.

"Suppose there is a righteous man who does what is just and right... He does not oppress anyone, but returns what he took in pledge for a loan.... He follows my decrees and faithfully keeps my laws. That man is righteous; he will surely live, declares the Sovereign LORD." - Ezekiel 18:5-9

Reading the entire chapter shows the full list of righteous behavior, but notice that a righteous person "returns what he took in pledge for a loan." If you want to be righteous, get out of debt, no matter how messed up your living conditions are. That is the call from God. Later in that chapter, Ezekiel repeats the same list stating that the person who does not do these things will be in for a rude awakening. In fact, the warning about not paying your debt (among other sins) culminates in this verse; **"Will such a man live? He will not! Because he has done all these detestable things, he will surely be put to death and his blood will be on his own head"** (Ezekiel 18:13). Not paying back debt is one of the behaviors that God labels as **"detestable things."**

If you are still in debt, the main questions you really need to take time to ponder have to do with your sense of urgency about your debt. Ask yourself the following:

- Am I really making every effort to get out of debt?

- Am I making sure I am getting out of debt without becoming greedy?

- Is my thinking about debt lined up with what the Bible says about debt?

- Would Jesus be pleased with the way I spend money and think about money?

Interesting Fact about Interest

The world we live in is governed by rules so unlike the rules in the Bible, that it is a wonder that anything good at all gets accomplished today. Take for instance the practice of banks charging interest for loans. Under most laws, such a practice is entirely legal and even strongly encouraged to grow the economy. However, what the Bible says about charging interest might shock you as well.

"If you lend money to one of my people among you who is needy, do not be like a moneylender; charge him no interest." - Exodus 22:25

God's plan for a holy nation involves lending without charging interest. Can you imagine that? **"No interest."** God does not want his people taken advantage of and exploited. What a wonderful world it would be.

Note that in the Old Testament, God did allow lending with interest to foreigners (Deuteronomy 23:19-20) but remember that any foreign male back then could enter the covenant and become one of God's people through circumcision. Today, of course, anyone can enter God's covenant too. God always provides a way for his creation to get close to him.

Money can get in the way of that closeness when we start to care more about money than God. The way God thinks about money is so different than how we consider it. Cancelling debt and not charging interest are concepts quite different from what we are used to today--bankers might even call it dangerous and absurd. Yet it is all the more reason to admire God for his care and wise direction toward his people. He does not want us to be slaves to money.

Stop the Money Madness

Most people know that the Great Recession of 2008 sucked people deeper into already existing debt. This is nothing new. The writing was on the wall already.

According to Newsweek's 8/27/2001 issue, **"Sixty percent of American families actually spend more than their after tax income..."** What does that mean? Put simply, most families spend more than they make. How can that possibly be good? We are talking about the majority of families taking up residence in the state of debt. They gambled with their future, and about a decade later, the pain is fully realized.

- Has your spending put your family at risk?

- Stop the spending madness and respect God's commands about debt.

"Let no debt remain outstanding, except the continuing debt to love one another, for he who loves his fellowman has fulfilled the law."
- Romans 13:8

- God wants your debt to be over and done with. Only one debt should remain: you owe it to love one another.

- Getting out of financial debt is a command.

- If you get a monthly letter or phone call from creditors hounding you to pay your debt, that stands out! It is an "outstanding" debt that God wants you to have a plan to get out of.

- Contact your creditors. Negotiate, plead, and even beg for them to agree on a realistic way for you to resolve your outstanding debt as quickly as possible. I have a few friends who have done this with creditors and it resulted in these friends paying way less if they could pay off the debt quicker.

- God does not want you to let your outstanding debt continue.

- God wants to own you as his dear child. He does not want anyone else taking ownership of you through the manipulative temptations and cold chains that come from being in debt.

The NASB translation of Romans 13:8 is even more direct. It says to **"Owe nothing to anyone...."** Notice the absolute choice of wording: "Owe nothing," as in "not anything at all." Not being in debt to "anyone" includes "everyone." In other words, biblically, there is no one, not even a family member, whom it is acceptable to be indebted to for any material thing at all for an extended period of time. This must become your new view of financial transactions and other material goods. A right understanding of this verse should help you think twice about every purchase or deal you may otherwise be inclined to make. The rest of the world does not think like this, but the days of "buy now, pay much later," must come to a close.

So what will it take for you to get out of debt and/or stay out of debt? Hopefully by now you are ready to attack and deal with your debt. Reposition yourself to "owe nothing to anyone..." except the lifelong debt to love one another.

Seven Actions Steps to Debt-Freedom

Below are some challenging, yet essential things you should do on the path to becoming debt-free. Some of the steps are actually things that you must do, as in completing a set of tasks. Yet most of these steps are more about who you must become. This is a process, and if you want the process to be initiated in your life, you must write these steps down, review them daily, and track your progress.

Please do not be surprised that these steps are challenging. If getting out of debt were easy, no one would be in debt. Some items described below will take a great degree of self-discipline to implement, and you may be tempted to skip a few steps, but do not do that. Remember that **"...with God, all things are possible"** (Matthew 19:26). Therefore combine your faith and deeds (James 2:14-26), as I believe that you need to incorporate all of these action steps together in order to succeed.

ACTION STEP 1) Don't serve money.

"No one can serve two masters. Either he will hate the one and love the other, or he will be devoted to the one and despise the other. You cannot serve both God and Money."
- Matthew 6:24

- Winning the fight to becoming free of debt must first be fought within your mind. In attacking the debt in your life, do not be overly consumed with thinking about money: especially money that you do not even possess.

Such thinking leads to distraction and worry, which is faithlessness.

- Keep a godly perspective by putting God first (Matthew 6:33) because it is biblically impossible to serve God and money. Don't be deceived at the ambiguity of statements like "put God first." You might ask, "What does that really mean?" The concept of putting God first seems abstract, vague, and even easy when you are not actually reading and following the scriptures daily. But when God becomes your priority, buckle up! That is when life really gets fascinating as he reveals more of his remarkable will to you.

- When you overspend and get into debt, you run the risk of serving money. Why? Because debt can bring worries and family fights that can enslave you into foolish patterns. Money becomes your master. You will work more hours and bring that added pressure into your home life. The end result is that you end up serving money and not the people you really care about.

- Beware of serving money. If you serve money, you are despising God.

- Putting the pursuit of money over your relationship with God is basically telling God that he is not so special, while money becomes the center of your life.

- If you are heavily in debt, and believe that you do love God over money, test yourself. Ask yourself, "Do I get more excited about praying to God or more excited to dream about how I can acquire more cash?" Another great question is, "Am I more eager to read my Bible or more interested in reading/listening to other things?"

- Money will never love you back, while **"God is love"** (1 John 4:8). That is who he is: a person full of love and the source of love. Therefore serve God with gladness and love.

ACTION STEP 2) Get help from a great leader.

You need a leader who walks the walk in finances and in faithfulness. Such a person is one to follow. A historical example of this can be found in the people who came to a certain man-on-the-run: the Israelite David, long before he was king.

"David left Gath and escaped to the cave of Adullam. When his brothers and his father's household heard about it, they went down to him there. All those who were in distress or in debt or discontented gathered around him, and he became their leader. About four hundred men were with him."
- 1 Samuel 22:1-2

- People in debt need to seek great leadership and mentoring to get out of debt. Those with David were willing to do something radical about their living situation (including their debt). Are you? Talk to mature, trusted and respected people in your life... repeatedly. Walk with them. I am not talking about financial advisers or brokers who take a cut of your investments. These folks do have to make a living, and I am sure some of them are helpful. Yet for the purpose of getting spiritual financial direction, I am talking about getting talk time with unbiased, financially stable, and faithful leaders you know very well who are not trying to make money off of you.

- These indebted people who first came to David would go on to become the future leaders and mighty men of God.

- Those with David were in a CAVE; that sounds uncomfortable. To get out of debt, you have got to get out of your comfort zone. How uncomfortable are you willing to become to get out of your debt?

- Doing what comes easily to you does not usually equate with what will make for a good income; that is why they call it "work," because it is hard. I know this firsthand. In college, I liked T-shirts and drawing (still do). So I spent $1,000 on silkscreen printer equipment, printed a few hundred shirts, and sold only 10 shirts in two years time.

Needless to say, my basement screen printing business did not have a good return on investment. Plus the ventilation in my makeshift basement print shop was horrible. I am sure I took at least a year or two off of my life from inhaling all the toxic ink fumes. What I needed to do was get out of my comfort zone and find out if there was even a viable market for what my skills were. There was not, so I got a job--any job that paid good money--and that funded my creative work.

"The way of a fool seems right to him, but a wise man listens to advice." - Proverbs 12:15

- Do not be a "fool." Get specific advice about your spending.

- If even people who are wise go and get advice, shouldn't you too?

- If you consider yourself wise, yet you do not get advice about your finances, then are you really as wise as you think you are? Remember what God says; the wise listen to advice.

ACTION STEP 3) Deny self.

When we talk about biblical self denial, we are talking about saying "no" to what we want, and "yes" to what God wants. Think of Jesus right before going to the cross, in the Garden of Gethsemane, praying to the Father: **"...not my will, but yours be done"** (Luke 22:42). Self denial is one of the hardest attitudes to maintain, and it makes or breaks most people. But it is so worth it to live a life of self denial; this pleases God. Notice too that, according to Jesus, denying self is not optional.

"...If anyone would come after me, he must deny himself..."
- Luke 9:23

- Often debt is a result of undisciplined living, which includes undisciplined spending. This is an unwillingness to deny self.

- Living beyond your means is selfish, because it is short-sighted. Such spending often hurts us and the people we are closest to. Consider what would please God in every situation. That thinking alone will alter your spending patterns if you know the Lord.

- Practice self-discipline without complaining. Resist the desire to cave in to your every whim. That is pathetic, cowardly and uninspiring.

A great way to deny self is to understand how to do something else Jesus says: to count the costs. In Luke 14:28, Jesus is explaining what it takes to follow him. He compares it to a person building a tower. One practical point from his story is how the potential builder should first sit down and estimate the cost before he starts building. I have never built a tower, but even in the old days, I am sure such a structure was not simply thrown together on a stroke of impulse. Building takes planning and time consuming consideration. In other words, think it through with careful detail before you commit to following Jesus. Know what is expected prior to jumping in.

This principle can also be applied to spending. Estimate how your potential purchases will impact your future economic stability. In Jesus' story from Luke 14, the builder actually could not finish the tower, and he was ridiculed. Doesn't this sound similar to how many people feel about their debt? They hide it and put up a good front. To avoid the ridicule of poverty, many scramble to multiple credit cards and unwise loans. The more we go back to denying self and counting the costs, the less we will be trapped by such schemes.

ACTION STEP 4) Be shrewd with money.

"I am sending you out like sheep among wolves. Therefore be as shrewd as snakes and as innocent as doves." - Matthew 10:16

Being shrewd is a command. The Blue Letter Bible defines "shrewd" as being wise, intelligent, prudent, mindful. The Oxford Dictionary defines "shrewd" as "having sharp powers of judgment, astute." Are you prudent with your spending? Prudent means "acting with or showing care and thought for the future" (Oxford Dictionary). Is this how you think about every one of your financial transactions? Again, Jesus commands shrewdness. Just a few examples of shrewd spending follow in the list below.

- When possible, barter for what you need. If you have stuff, a skill, or provide a specialized service, try to offer that in trade for the service or item you need. For example, as a publisher, it is common for me to give books away free in return for free publicity. On a more domestic front, once I traded my collection of old Lionel model trains for a new stove and refrigerator. Yes, you heard that right. We avoided a $1,000 bill.

- Network frequently to be always looking for a higher paying job (even if you already have a job). Do not let this practice consume you, but also do not get comfortable in any secular job. My guideline is this: even if you have a decent job, spend an hour per week exploring higher paying potential jobs. Then network with people who are in that industry or company. Think about it this way, somewhere in your city, it is likely that a similar person is doing a job similar to yours, yet for higher wages. Find that person, and find that job.

- Buying fresh fruit and vegetables for snacks instead of processed junk food snacks will save you a hundreds of dollars each year. What is processed junk food? If it is not in the fruit and vegetable section of the grocery store, and it is in a bag or box with a fancy design, it is most likely junk food (which will also make you fat).

- Eat peanuts. This food is often associated with poverty, as in "My employer is so cheap; they are barely paying me peanuts!" While peanuts do not have the greatest reputation, they are actually quite nutritious and yes, they are very cheap. They make for an excellent snack and are loaded with protein.

- If you can get something for free, do not pay for it. This might seem obvious but I know plenty of people who will buy an expensive cup of coffee every weekday at Starbucks (or any cafe) on the way to the office. How is this a waste? Most offices offer coffee for their workers in the break room--for free. That is over $20 per week.

- Seek free samples. Here is an example that shows how you can be creative with free samples. My wife and I would infrequently have what we would call "free sample dates." As you might imagine, these dates would involve us going out to a grocery store or gallery opening and sampling as much free food as the places would put out on display. We sort of made a sport out of the activity, and had lots of fun. They continue to be memorable dates.

- Pack a lunch rather than pay to eat out. For school or work, make your lunch the night before. I am not saying to *never* eat out, but reducing the frequency will help tremendously. It can save you hundreds of dollars a month. The issue really comes down to how quickly you want to get out of debt.

- If you get sick of eating food from your home, get creative with the food. Often you can do this at no extra cost by turning the food into unique forms.

- If you go to a restaurant, avoid going when you are really hungry. I realize that this point needs some explanation because it sounds ridiculous at first. When I know I am going to a restaurant to pay for food, I will try to eat a little something from home first before I leave for the restaurant. That way, if I eat a piece of bread, or a handful of nuts beforehand, then I will not show up to the restaurant with a growling stomach. Therefore, I train my mind to order less food. Less food equals less money spent. The other night my wife and I did this, and we got by on just ordering an appetizer. It tasted great and we still had the experience of someone else cooking for us. If you plan this right, you can go out to eat for one third the expense. I am not saying to do this every time you go to a restaurant, but the more you do this, the more you save.

- When eating a meal out, do not buy your beverage. Have water or bring your own. If you are not crazy about always having plain water, try carbonated water. Many restaurants with a self-service drink fountain will let you have carbonated water for free, just like tap water.

- Contact your insurance company (car, home) every few years to see if you can get the bill lowered. Ask them to explain to you line by line what exactly you are paying for. Do you really need all that coverage? Repeat this every time you have to renew coverage.

- Use a bicycle, walk, or take public transportation when possible.

- If you have to buy something, see if you can get it used, rather than new.

- Do not buy a book or a DVD that you can borrow or use from the library for free. How many times can you really watch the same movie?

- Give up dinner once a week. Meal portions are so big in America, that most people could probably split their lunch in half and eat a portion in the afternoon and a portion for dinner. I learned this from my friend Raja who was visiting from India. He was continually amazed at the size of the meal portions that were served here. When he received his order at one modest fast food restaurant in Chicago, he leaned over to me and said with astonishment, "Wow, this plate could feed two people in my country--maybe even three!" Because of this, our family frequently looks for what one thing at a restaurant we can order and then split it between us. It all adds up.

- Make a budget of your current spending patterns. You cannot make cuts if you do not know where all your money is going. Track your spending for at least three months; save every receipt from every purchase. Factor in any annual bills and this should give you a decent snapshot of your financial patterns. Under every expense ask, "Do I need this?" or "Do I need all of this? What can I cut?" You might be surprised, and hopefully alarmed at what money is being wasted. Identify it and put a stop to it. I was tracking our monthly spending on food for a few months and discovered that we, as a family of four, were spending $600 per month on food. For some, that might sound like a lot of money, but it comes out to $20 per day for a family of four. That is not so bad. But I wanted to see if we could get it lower. So we came up with a new plan. Instead of going to the grocery store once a week, we would go once every two weeks. This forced us to prepare more food, eat less boxed and processed junk, and amazingly cut our food bill by $250 dollars--almost in half! That comes out to $3,000 in annual savings.

- Avoid budget pride. This is where the person is so confident that they know their own bills and spending patterns, that they refuse to really make a detailed budget, yet wonder why they are more broke than they thought they would be. Keep in mind that a new budget, especially if you have never done one before, will take about three hours to create. Put in the time, and you will avoid wasting the money.

- Do not buy gifts. You should still give gifts, but see if you can make the gift, write a nice card, or give something that you already own. My old comic book collection (before I sold it) was a great source of gifts for kids, teens, and like-minded adults over the years. I am certain that this principle has saved us thousands of dollars over the past decade. One year my wife made soap for everyone. Who does not use soap? Even if the recipient does not like the gift, eventually, they will still put it to good use. It is soap.

- Not everything that is broken needs to be fixed. It may be nice to spend money to fix it, but when something breaks, ask yourself, "Can I still use this item in its broken state?" If not, then ask, "Can I do without this item if I do not replace or repair it?" For example, we had a broken light on our downstairs stairwells for almost 15 years. For a while we talked about paying an electrician to fix it, but we soon learned to just walk in the dark in that area of the house. We benefited in three ways from this decision:
1) The family learned not to be afraid of the dark.
2) We learned to walk with a ninja-style sweeping motion so as not to trip on anything unseen. How cool is that?
3) Unfixed broken things can save us money.

- Baked goods also make great gifts. One year, our family took large plain cookies and decorated them with colored icing. On a number of the cookies, I even drew with icing the likeness of the person who was getting the cookie. Giving food as a gift has been common throughout history. And on the very low budget side, write them a series of notes and slip them into fortune cookies. Heartfelt letters are always memorable as well.

- Found objects can also make good gifts. Sometimes I find flat rocks or sea glass, draw on them, and give them away as presents. If you cannot draw you can still write something nice on these neat objects--they make great paperweights and tokens of affection.

On a regular basis, review and even memorize scriptures that specifically talk about money. There are so many of them, you'll run out of memory before you run out of scriptures. Still, use these verses to direct the course of your financial ponderings and dealings.

"Of what use is money in the hand of a fool, since he has no desire to get wisdom?"
- Proverbs 17:16

- Do not be a fool with money. That is useless. Today we have a more socially acceptable word for this: materialism, but it is still just as foolish to be materialistic. The desire for things and money is quite destructive in the hands of a fool. Being a wise spender is about being shrewd. Ask yourself how Jesus would allocate each portion of your paycheck.

- Some people may think that being a shrewd spender might be contrary to being charitable. However, that is not necessarily true. You can be a shrewd spender, but still be generous. That is where denying self comes in. The key is spending only on essential items for you, your ministry, and your family. Then you will find that there will be even more money for God's work and for others in need.

This is not merely an untested hypothesis of mine. Frugal spending on yourself makes generosity even more possible. For many years, I have had only one pair of blue jeans. My spring coat was from three decades ago. Aside from dress shoes, I'm content to wear shoes long past the point of them having a few minor holes. This might sound extreme, but how many outfits did Jesus have?

Applying frugality to daily living has made it possible to increase our level of charitable giving into the thousands of dollars for many years. I say this not at all to boast, but only to demonstrate what is doable with godly planning, wisdom, and discipline. Remember all those computer gadgets I did not buy? All that money added up to us being able to buy a brand new computer for a friend who leads our sister church in India. Godly frugality can have a global impact.

ACTION STEP 5) Repent and pray

"...The prayer of a righteous man is powerful and effective."
- James 5:16

How effective are your prayers? If your answer is "not so much," then increase your faith and your doing of God's will. That is what righteousness is about: doing what is right in

God's eyes, not our own. Righteous prayer warriors are effective. And warriors are powerful!

I was reading about the resurrection of Jesus one morning in Matthew 28, and it was powerful. I noticed something I never really appreciated before. There is an earthquake, not just any earthquake, but a violent one. Then an angel comes down and rolls away the stone over Jesus' tomb. The angel had an appearance similar to lightning, and his clothes were as white as snow.

Now some might read this account and think, "Wow, that is so cool! Angels must be like super heroes. That angel must be like Storm, from the X-Men, combined with the Silver Surfer. I wish I could have seen that angel. Perhaps it might even be easier to imagine the sight today, especially with all the special effects in movies that make supernatural events and characters appear so real. However, what struck me when I read the resurrection passage this morning was the reaction of the guards at the tomb. The Bible says that they were so afraid of the angel that they shook and became like dead men! The very presence of this angel was terrifying. Even Mary Magdalene, who was also there, was afraid.

What does this have to do with prayer? It occurred to me, after I read this passage and started praying, that I was not just praying to anyone. I was praying to the all-powerful God who created that angel. If God can dream up and then create such an angel whose very existence causes some to become as if dead, then surely God is more than capable of answering my prayers. This understanding spurred me on to pray even more fervently. Shouldn't we all?

- The word "pray" and its offshoots, prayer, praying, etc., are in the Bible 365 times. Not coincidentally, that is one for each day of the year. Pray specifically and regularly about your finances--that God gives you wisdom to manage them in a way that would please him. Ask God to help you see the greed in your heart that got you in debt in the first place, and Beg for a willing spirit of repentance. Talk to God daily.

- Do not just pray; Repent and pray. God answers all sorts of prayers, but he makes special note of prayers from those who do his will. That is the righteous. In other words, those who do what is proper in the eyes of God are the righteous. Their prayers are "effective." There are many key components to righteousness. One of the big ones is repentance.

- What is repentance? It means to turn. Learn what God says is evil and then stop doing that evil; turn the other way, towards the good. For a list of sins in the Bible, see Galatians 5:19-21 as well as 2 Timothy 3:1-5. There are actually many other lists of evil deeds in the scriptures, but the above two are a good place to start. Use a dictionary to look up each word listed in these scriptures as a sin and see how they apply to your life. Take drastic measures to change. That will keep you occupied for quite some time.

"I was young and now I am old, yet I have never seen the righteous forsaken or their children begging bread." - Psalm 37:25

This is such a loaded verse. It describes the pattern of those who live a life of repentance and trust in God. Notice what happens to the righteous; they are never abandoned by God or in economic trouble so deep that their kids have to beg for food. Here is a wake-up call from God for so many; people want to be out of debt, yet they are unwilling to say no to their own greed and other evils. We all need to live a life of repentance from acts that lead to death. The answer for all of us is to stop doing things by our own power and follow *the will of God,* which is the definition of righteousness. Surrender to God's plan. His wisdom is greater than yours. Whose plan got you into debt? Your plan. Drop that plan. Start following God's plan.

Jesus did not live a flashy life with all the comforts of the day. He left the wonder, riches, and security of paradise to exist with us as a fellow man with all the weakness and fragility that comes from being in our mortal bodies on this earth. Then he says "follow me," throughout the New Testament. We are not called to a life of riches, but to a life in the care of the good shepherd. He gives the righteous what they need. Therefore, put your life in God's hands. What does such a life look like? It involves praying with faith--believing you will receive what you are asking for with right motives. Prayer combined with repentance is where you want to be. As previously discussed from James 5:16, **"...The prayer of a righteous man is powerful and effective."** There is no quick pill you can take to instantly make you prayerful. There is no ointment you can put on to make you righteous overnight. Prayer and righteousness come the old fashioned way--through blood, sweat, and even tears in obedience to the word of God.

Mega-Faithful

Repenting of faithlessness is another major area of focus that must be addressed. Have you ever seen a word used so much, that after a while you tune the meaning out because of the frequency and volume of its use? I believe that the word "faith" is one of those words. Being faithful is discussed quite often in matters concerning God: so much so, that when others remind you to "be faithful," it does not really register because you have heard that phrase a million and one times.

Many people have lost faith in God. They are disappointed in him because he did not give them what they wanted when they wanted it. Consequently they are faithless. They do not believe God can help them anymore, so they stop praying. Or they pray as a formality, but with no trust that God will take seriously their request. That is faithlessness, and it must be repented of quickly. God is God. He can guide you to get a better job. He can help you have the self-discipline to not overspend. He can provide amazing opportunities that you never imagined. But you must follow him--with faith.

Therefore, to really believe this, what everyone needs to do, is to consciously focus on what faith means, and constantly protect, guard, and build up that faith. It takes mental discipline, but it is so worth it. I recall many years ago, I was at risk of being laid off due to budget cuts, and in an overly anxious tone, I asked my friend Juan what was I going to do? Indignantly, Juan replied, "God can get you a job. It is silly to think that such a thing is outside of his power--God can do anything! But that is not the issue; the issue is that you need faith to believe that God will help you in this area."

My friend was right, and it took that blunt conversation to snap me out of my faithless line of thinking. I began to value my faith much more after that talk, because right after I boosted my faith, the funding cuts were fixed and my job stabilized. In retrospect, I realize how mentally undisciplined I had become about my faith, and I really needed to value it so much more on a daily basis.

That is why Paul says to **"fight the good fight of the faith"** (1 Timothy 6:12), because it really is a daily battle to retain and expand upon our faith. People know how to fight the good fight for their career. Everyone fights the fight to get money, but are we working that hard to fight for our faith? We must fight all the rest of the days of our lives--for our faith.

In Luke 18:8 we discover what Jesus puts his value and great attention toward. It is so different than what the rest of the world is seeking, yet it is so very right! **"When the Son of Man comes, will he find faith on the earth?"**

Jesus left paradise to come here; he could go anywhere and be looking for whatever his heart desires. But his sole desire was (and still is) to look for one specific characteristic in people. Reading the gospels, you will see that he was singularly searching for a certain quality of mankind. Jesus was looking for people of faith. That should show you how much Jesus values faith. Are you like Jesus, prioritizing the search for faith, or more like the rest of the world, looking for money as of first importance?

You will run into all kinds of challenges in this life that will test and try to destroy your faith, or at least confuse your faith. These are the trials of life. Essentially, the devil is out to rob you of your faith. He knows, as we should, that faith is more valuable than money. So each person really needs to ask this question daily; if Jesus were to return today, would he find me faithful?

There is no room for excuses. All people will fall into one of two categories at Jesus' return. Either you will be found faithful: that is, hoping with certainty that the scriptures are true and that by faith, your life actions are in one accord with the scriptures. Or you will be found unfaithful: that is, not believing the words of God, and doing your own thing with your time and your money. The choice is yours to make, and you cannot use the excuses of life being too hard, or that you have suffered too much to hold onto a biblical level of faith. Jesus is still coming and he is looking for people who have faith.

Regarding these trials and the suffering of this life, 1 Peter 1:6-7 explains that these trials **"...have come so that your faith--of greater worth than gold, which perishes even though refined by fire--may be proved genuine and may result in praise, glory and honor when Jesus Christ is revealed."**

See the emphasis and dominant importance of faith here? Take away a few nuggets from this passage. Gold will perish. As permanent and sought after as it may seem, gold will not last. Yet faith is worth more and greater than gold.

Gold is greatly valued, and has been from ancient times, yet the Bible gives gold an expiration date; it will perish. Most of the world does not view it this way. If you had gold, you would value and protect that completely. You would be inspired to do some amazing deeds if you had access to hidden gold, or if someone were trying to steal your gold. Face it, you would be up in arms. That is how you need to treat your faith! Your Christian faith is to be treasured and protected at all costs and above all things. It is the most valuable thing you possess. Upon Jesus' return, I pray that he finds you and me faithful!

To help myself remember the priceless value of faith, I wrote a little jingle. I believe it will strengthen you too. It is called "Faith Much More than Gold."

Faith is worth much more than gold.
This is the truth I will uphold.
Faith is worth much more than gold.

Must remember or your heart will get cold.
Faith is worth much more than gold.
Jesus said it to Peter, now we've been told.
Faith is worth much more than gold.
Don't forget it, even when you're old.

ACTION STEP 6) Participate in Holy Spending

There is another aspect of God and money that defies logic, yet is completely true. It has to do with what you give to God, and what you do not give to him. See this passage from Malachi about tithing, which means giving a tenth of your income back to God.

"'Return to me, and I will return to you,' says the LORD Almighty. 'But you ask, "How are we to return?" Will a man rob God? Yet you rob me. But you ask, "How do we rob you?" In tithes and offerings. You are under a curse-- the whole nation of you--because you are robbing me. Bring the whole tithe into the storehouse, that there may be food in my house. Test me in this,' says the LORD Almighty, 'and see if I will not throw open the floodgates of heaven and pour out so much blessing that you will not have room enough for it. I will prevent pests from devouring your crops, and the vines in your fields will not cast their fruit,' says the LORD Almighty. 'Then all the nations will call you blessed, for yours will be a delightful land,' says the LORD Almighty." - Malachi 3: 7-12

Some might be thinking, "Hold on there. I need to *reduce* my expenses, not add expenses to my budget. Giving away a tenth of what I earn will never get me out of debt!" I do understand this line of thinking and have even followed it in the past. Yet what God says is solid. He says to test him in your giving of a tenth, and he will **"pour out so much blessing that you will not have room enough for it."** If you believe the word of God, then you will get your finances in the proper order so you can tithe.

A word of caution though is needed here; there are so many false churches out there that the majority of people who try tithing think they are giving to God, yet because they are in a religious organization where Jesus is the leader in name only, their money never advances God's true movement. Therefore, they are not really giving to God and so they miss out on the blessings associated with God's plan.

Nevertheless, tithing in a true church led by Jesus Christ should be done out of gratitude and love for God. Look at the byproduct of such giving; it brings holy protection upon your economic plans. As God says in Malachi 3, **"I will prevent pests from devouring your crops, and the vines in your fields will not cast their fruit."**

To be "holy" means to be sacred, set aside for a special purpose, dedicated to God. You are commanded by God to be holy, because he is holy (1 Peter 1:16). Since so much of what we do to exist on this earth involves the use of money, we must develop holy spending patterns. It is part of the "being holy" process. We must be holy with our money. Therefore, giving generously to God's church and to the poor are the very concrete and direct ways to participate in holy spending.

Time and time again my wife and I have observed this firsthand. We tithe and what God has poured out from his floodgates has been remarkable; I received two raises in the same year, one of which I did not even ask for. On top of that, my wife then got a writing gig earning in three weeks what would have taken me three months to make. Again, she did not seek this opportunity. It sought her. Moreover, when I started working on the very beginnings of this book, our house was not completely paid for. Yet as stated earlier, by the time I finished this book, with much gratitude, I can report that our house has been completely paid off, sold for a profit, and now we live in a place nicer than I could have ever imagined.

How have all these things fallen into place? It is certainly not by our own power. It is God--working the floodgates as we gave by faith over the years. Thank you God!

Of course, we do not give to God so that we can receive all these nice things. We certainly enjoy them, but we give to God out of gratitude for what he has done for us. We give out of a deep belief and confidence that God Almighty is worth so much more than we can ever repay. We give out of our love for him. We give because we fully support (in word and deed) the advancement of his exceedingly good news. Set aside your finances for God. Get holy with your spending!

Another biblical way to get holy with your spending is to be generous to others. This is repeatedly described in Proverbs 11:24-25. **"One man gives freely, yet gains even more; another withholds unduly, but comes to poverty. A generous man will prosper; he who refreshes others will himself be refreshed."**

Notice the emphasis on giving and generosity. God links being generous to prosperity and personal refreshment. This too is holy spending. Again, it defies simple arithmetical logic because on a balance sheet, money going outwards decreases the bottom line. But God works outside the confines of a spreadsheet. On a supernatural level, he guides the givers to **"gain even more."** Through our faith in the workings of God, he magnifies our giving. Remember that God is not regulated by any stock market, monetary fund, global financial institution, or government currency board. He can do whatever he wants with money. It is refreshing to see that he is the authority behind the call for us to be holy spenders. Participate now in holy spending.

ACTION STEP 7) Please God

"A man can do nothing better than to eat and drink and find satisfaction in his work. This too, I see, is from the hand of God, for without him, who can eat or find enjoyment? To the man who pleases him, God gives wisdom, knowledge and happiness, but to the sinner he gives the task of gathering and storing up wealth to hand it over to the one who pleases God. This too is meaningless, a chasing after the wind."
- Ecclesiastes 2:24-26

This verse from Ecclesiastes is about 3,000 years old, yet still just as true today as it ever was. Notice the use of the phrase **"nothing better"** in the first verse. We learn that finding satisfaction in our work is an essential best-practice in employment. In other words, there is **"nothing better."** This does not mean to immediately quit your job for a better one. It means whatever job you have, learn how to get satisfaction from it. Find the good in it; be grateful for the opportunity. When that happens, you will outperform others and that is where the happiness comes, along with an eventual raise or promotion. Of course, if a more rewarding job is discovered in the course of time, by all means take it.

Breaking down the rest of the passage reveals a truth that will be disturbing for those who know they are not living a life that honors God right now. To the person who is not pleasing God with how they live due to unrepentant sin, God **"gives the task of gathering and storing up wealth to hand it over to**

the one who pleases God." In other words, there are hard-working, financially successful people out there right now in a boatload of sin and ignorant of God's ways. They will continue to get rich up to a point. Yet some time later, God will literally move these rich people to **"hand it over"** to you if you are pleasing God.

Therefore be urgent to please God, not because it is the secret to receiving wealth, but because pleasing God is good for your relationship with him. Then as a by-product, at some point in the future, material wealth may come your way in the form of an inheritance, a gift, or other circumstance that God determines.

Yet be warned; if you stop pleasing God, your newfound wealth can just as easily be handed over to another person who is currently making God happy by their reverent lifestyle. Again, the focus is not to adopt this as a get-rich-quick scheme. The intent is to be in a great relationship with God where both parties find enjoyment: you and God together. With the Bible as your blueprint, you can **"find out what pleases the Lord"** (Ephesians 5:10), and happiness will come to you.

Action Step Review (Now Put It Into Practice)

The 1980s pop singer Cyndi Lauper sang with great zeal how "Money Changes Everything!" Less lauded, but equally true, is the notion that understanding, with faith and discipline, can change everything too. Hopefully you will reflect on these debt-busting principles, and swiftly put them into action. However, if you merely reflect on these concepts, yet do not put any of them into practice, your situation will not change--it may even get worse.

Now you have a road map with biblical guidelines, and the path to getting out of debt should be more defined. Moreover, you should conclude that these action steps are right-on and not risky. They are not rocket science. The challenge at hand is to live by them. Make them who you are. I am certain that once you do so, your only regret will be, "I just wish I would have started this lifestyle sooner."

1) Do not serve money.
2) Get help from a great leader.
3) Deny self.
4) Be shrewd with money.
5) Repent and pray.
6) Participate in Holy Spending.
7) Please God.

Take note that there are seven action steps. Write each action step down on a separate index card and assign it to a recurring day of the week. Focus on the application of one of these action steps per day. For example, you might assign the action step "Repent and pray" to every Monday. Meditate on this throughout the entire day and take fitting action.

Yes, I know, the reality is that we all have to apply every action step together daily to have lasting victory. But for those just getting started at these concepts, you must build up to it day by day or it might seem overwhelming. That is why it is best to focus on one action step per day on a weekly recurring basis. That fact that there are seven action steps, and seven days of the week, is no accident. Daily application of change is what it takes to untangle yourself from the sad mess that comes with debt and greed.

Remember, you are changing the course of a river. It represents years of bad spending patterns. Results will not be evident overnight. But you must be in the godly debt-busting mindset for life. Then, with God, patience, prayer and discipline, you can bust out from under the shackles of your creditors and **finally become debt-free!**

Lazy Enough

When speaking of repentance of the behaviors and circumstances that led you into debt, we must address a sin that most people in debt must repent of quickly before your money pit and the indentation in your couch gets any deeper: **laziness**. I am probably hitting a nerve right here, pretty certain that some people hearing this will suddenly stop listening. Some might be inclined to get defensive right away and say that they work so hard at their job and at home; how dare anyone call them lazy! Let me clarify. I am not suggesting that you are lazy in everything. However, what any person in debt must examine is whether or not they are working hard in the wrong job because they became comfortable there and are too lazy to put in the hard work it takes to look for a better paying job. In other words, you might be mostly a hard worker, but *lazy enough* to let certain things slide. It is not that you are an all-out lazy bum; yet truth be told, you are just lazy enough to remain in debt.

What I am talking about is lazy-mindedness. That is where a person does not have the integrity to face the truth of reality: that they must suffer to look for a higher salary. That takes time and effort. Perhaps they should not come home and watch a movie to unwind. Perhaps instead, they come home from a hard day at work, pray for a while, eat, and then resume their job search. Perhaps on their lunch break, instead of taking that refreshing walk, they tough it out, pray for strength, and use that free time to look for other jobs. It is a sacrifice. That is why repenting of laziness takes extreme mental discipline.

Let us see what the Bible says about the lazy. The word "sluggard" is often used in the Bible to describe a lazy person. A sluggard is a person who is habitually inactive. The word is synonymous with lazy, idler, do-nothing, loafer. As you might have guessed, this does not paint a pretty picture.

A pattern of debt often points to lazy-minded thinking. Again, let me remind you that I am not saying people are lazy across the board. But if there is longstanding debt, for your own sake, you must at least consider whether or not you might be lazy about this particular area of your life: being lazy-minded about finances: how you spend your money and what you do in your spare time.

Perhaps instead of looking for a better-paying job in your spare time, you just need to start working harder and more responsibly at your own job to raise up and become a manager (making more money). Managing has so much to do with how you think, how you treat people, and how you motivate them. This comes back to your mind. Become more self-disciplined with how you operate at work and you may be surprised to see who notices. God certainly will take note, as might your supervisor, whom God can give the power to call you into a higher paying position within the company.

"Go to the ant, you sluggard; consider its ways and be wise." Proverbs 6:6

This proverb about the ant is quite amazing in its simplicity yet power. Despite its tiny stature, the ant does not merely do random work that may or may not be useful. Rather, the ant does the right kind of work to get the right job done. The ant also leverages the work of other ants to increase the scope of its own work. God made the ant brilliantly to be a model of unity in efficiency. The Bible commands you to think about how the ant works.

Now overlap that with how you work. Is your work producing the necessary requirements to sustain you? If you are still in debt, the answer might be "no." The ways of the ant are calling you higher. Reexamine what job you are in, how you do that job, and if that particular job is really a vehicle for you to be the most effective you can be to produce appropriate income.

Consider one of my former employees. Let's call her Jane. She is amazing at her job, which is to place people with disabilities in jobs. Jane is so good at her job, that she ran circles around my other staff, outperforming them in almost every area. In fact, most days, I wish I had ten more staff like her.

Yet Jane has one little problem. She is bitter about life and therefore does not know how to inspire coworkers. In fact, she often mocks people without even being aware of it. It is stopping her from growing. I have brought it up to her multiple times. But she refuses to change. She is unwilling to dig deep and use the mental discipline it would take to deal with her bitter attitude. I have even told her that if she would change, she could be promoted and make more money. Moreover, she could even do my job when I leave the company, increasing her salary by over twenty five percent. But Jane is comfortable with her bitter attitude. That is all she knows. Therefore Jane is stuck in a lazy-minded cycle that will keep her in a low paying job--probably for the rest of her life.

Here is a perfect example of a hard worker who does her job, yet is lazy-minded about her behavior and therefore will never be considered for a promotion until she changes. What is so sad about this is that it is just one area of her behavior. Yet it does so much damage, it taints every other area of her life. In fact, other staff have accused her of being a racist because of her bitter, sometimes even angry spirit. But they do not understand the bigger picture. Jane is not racist; she is just mad at everyone. She is cynical toward God and bitter at life.

I have repeatedly offered to get help for Jane and train her how to get out of this pattern. But she is too comfortable with where she is at. And that is precisely the problem; comfortability (which is more socially acceptable) can be a clever yet damaging disguise for lazy-mindedness. In other words, if a person is comfortable with their behavior, there is no urgency to change. This comfortability, also known as lazy-mindedness, is stopping Jane, and it could be stopping you, from growing.

Consider this scripture to understand the dead end nature of someone who is lazy-minded at work. **"As vinegar to the teeth and smoke to the eyes, so is a sluggard to those who send him"** (Proverbs 10:26). My problem with Jane was that I could not count on her to train others to do what she does well at her job, because she continues to spread her negativity wherever she goes. Jane is a "sluggard" about her bitter attitude, and therefore she becomes "smoke to the eyes" of her supervisor (me). Why? Because new employees think that the bitter attitude of Jane, a seasoned employee is acceptable, and soon the impressionable new employee could imitate Jane's bitter attitude. This creates an even more toxic work environment, which is why Jane will never be considered for a higher paying position.

We all have a temptation to become physically lazy as well as lazy-minded. The world offers so many excuses to be lazy:

summer break, spring break, winter break, the weekend, lunch break, coffee break, happy hour, comfy couches, and more. I am not saying we should not take breaks. But use the breaks strategically. Be diligent about getting out of debt in some of these breaks.

The Bible shows us a stark contrast between the sluggard and the diligent. **"The sluggard craves and gets nothing, but the desires of the diligent are fully satisfied"** (Proverbs 13:4). If you have a lot of unfulfilled cravings, you may not be diligent with how you spend money and how to make more of it in a godly manner. Notice that "the desires of the diligent are fully satisfied." That means God takes care of those who are diligent. To be diligent is to show care and conscientiousness in work or duties. It is more than hard work. It is working carefully with an awareness of what is right. In other words, it is working hard at the most fitting job, not just working hard at any job. If this does not describe you, it may be time to shake up your life--seek diligent work.

Consider the following verse to get moving. **"The way of the sluggard is blocked with thorns, but the path of the upright is a highway."** - Proverbs 15:19

There are two kinds of people and two different paths. The lazy person is blocked by thorns while the upright person blazes down the highway. God influences which path we are on based on our attitude about him and about work. How you approach work defines which path you end up on. I have even seen two people on the same road under the same circumstances, and the person with faith blazes forward in victory while the person without faith gets lazy about the journey and even the smallest obstacles become thorns to them.

Will you surge or slump? The answer rests largely in how much you fight for your faith *plus* your level of diligence toward the work that you do. This is faith and deeds working in harmony. These two characteristics must work together, or they both become ineffective. As it says in James 2:26, **"...faith without deeds is dead."**

In Proverbs 19:24 we find something comical at first glance. **"The sluggard buries his hand in the dish; he will not even bring it back to his mouth!"** how humorous it is to imagine this scenario. The lazy person is so ineffectual that he does not even have the self discipline to bring his hand back to his mouth to eat. But this proverb is about us. There are things we get our hands on: things within our reach, things that we have been given the ability to accomplish. We even bury ourselves in such desires. Yet all too often, we refuse to muster the self discipline required to see the desire through to completion.

God is calling you to follow through on what is right. Stop being lazy-minded about the good you know you ought to do. The hardest part is getting started. Lift your hand out of the dish; get it done. For example, there have been periods in my life where I knew I needed to start looking for a job. The dead end of the current job had been revealed and it was time to move on. The knowledge of how to get a new and better job was all in my grasp--my hand was in the dish. I knew I needed to start networking with others in my desired industry, revising my resume, and doing the tedious extra work of filling out applications and writing personalized cover letters.

Yet all too often, this is where the sluggard mentality sets in. I rest my hand in this dish. I do not want to go through the mental suffering of actually doing the work it takes to find this new and better job. I would rather take a pleasant walk, or read, or even waste time on a video game to unwind. I just want to rest with my hand in the dish, holding onto the idea of a better job. Somewhere, it was just waiting for me, but I will never grasp it unless I am willing to suffer past the lazy thinking.

Repentance from this lazy-minded attitude is getting my hand out of the dish and seeing the task through to victory. It is called being a closer, as in "there is the person who can close the deal--make it happen." Is that who you are? Take inspiration from God, who is the ultimate closer; **"...he who began a good work in you will carry it on to completion until the day of Christ Jesus"** (Philippians 1:6). God sees things through until they are complete. He begins good and he follows through until there is final accomplishment. God does not get lazy-minded or distracted by other priorities. The good that he begins in his followers, he stays on task to ensure a solid victory.

Like God, we must all become closers to have victories. Let us be clear that victory is more than an idea you hold in your hand. Victory is something you fully digest. Close the deal. Let us repent of lazy-minded, go-nowhere dreams that never come true. Take part in fruitful labor that brings results. Endure the mental suffering, the thankless labor pains to see your goals go from an idea in a dish to a reality you can savor in your very own mouth.

Excuses may try to stop you once you get started on this path against laziness. There is no end to the excuses that can poison your mind. Yet do not give in to excuses. Proverbs 22:13 puts it most dramatically. **"The sluggard says, 'There is a lion outside!' or, 'I will be murdered in the streets!'"**

A sluggard is very skilled at inventing powerful excuses. They have the effect of instantly halting progress. Again, we must understand that most of the barriers we face that block progress are all in our mind. It goes back to lazy-minded thinking. The tired mind is not willing to internally oppose any negative excuses that it might be tempted with. Therefore the sluggard gives in to the illusion of caution when what is really happening is complacency.

Think about what has stopped you from growing? For many people, it is the dreaded paralysis of analysis. That is when there is too much thinking yet not enough appropriate work, and the thinking has a crippling effect. Once again, it goes back to what is going on in our thoughts: being lazy-minded. It is easier to spend way too much time thinking things to death. That is safer than actually taking action. Life is about taking risks. Think of all the risks Jesus took: he had no place to lay his head, walking on water, standing up to the religious hypocrites who were in power, pouring his efforts into people whom he knew would later betray him, getting arrested, tortured, and even killed. We are called to follow him. There is no room for lazy-mindedness in the path of Christ.

Proverbs 26:14 gives us another great illustration of the folly of being lazy. **"As a door turns on its hinges, so a sluggard turns on his bed."** Contemplate how inseparable a door and its hinges are. Anyone with a tendency to be lazy must completely remove himself from the trappings that foster more laziness. Just as a door is bound to the hinges, the sluggard is bound to lazy-minded thoughts. This is slavery. The only way to break free is to change how you think. Get up, get off the hinges, and get moving on what is right: godly thoughts that lead to results.

Take an objective view of your last few months. Is your life embarrassing because of laziness and debt? Or do you work hard--not simply at whatever job you happen to have--but work hard at getting the job that will help you get out of debt?

The non-lazy righteous life is one of generosity, giving to God and those in need. Follow the plan laid out in the Bible: a plan of repentance and prayer. Then you too can be righteous, pleasing the one who created the universe not by big spending, but by his will and his very word.

The-LORD-Is-With-You Factor

The following statement is not pretty, nor is it politically correct, yet I have found it to be true. If you are constantly in debt and God saves no one through your personal ministry, then God is most likely not with you. This is a biblical principle that can be readily seen in the life of the patriarch Joseph.

In Genesis 37, Joseph is a teenager, free and favored by his father Jacob. Young Joseph has a bold and unconventional dream: that his brothers and parents would be bowing down to him. Decades later, this happened just as Joseph dreamed, and in the future Joseph even becomes the number two leader in all of Egypt. Moreover, Joseph goes on to save many nations by his wisdom and faith in God. The young dreamer started life debt-free and finished it debt-free. That is something to admire, but such a life did not come easy, especially when considering Joseph's life from age 17 to 30; he falls victim to cruelty, crime, great injustice, and prison. I believe that the reason why God allowed Joseph such periods of freedom and prosperity later in life was because of Joseph's attitude during those times of intense hardship and even indebted servitude.

Let us review what happened after Joseph's teenage dreams. His brothers are so enraged by the thought of a future wherein they bow down and are indebted to their little brother that they come inches away from killing him. Then they sell him into slavery. Despite these troubles, as an Egyptian slave in Genesis 39, the LORD is with Joseph and blesses everything he does. That phrase is repeated several times. As you read the below verses and go about your own activities, you really have to examine what exactly you are involved in on a personal level and ask, "Is this a behavior that God would bless?"

- **"The LORD was with Joseph and he prospered..."** (Genesis 39:2)

- **"...the LORD gave him success in everything he did..."** (Genesis 39:3)

- **"...the LORD blessed the household of the Egyptian because of Joseph..."** (Genesis 39:5)

Notice the important details of Joseph's situation:
1) Joseph is a slave. He is owned; therefore he is in the most extreme form of debt.
2) God is with Joseph despite his lack of freedom. Since so many people today are slaves to their job and in debt without any end in sight, the question to ask is this; "Why was God so definitively with Joseph?"

The answer lies in the favor (grace) of God as well as understanding Joseph's personal character. Consider Joseph's commitment to purity. When the wife of Joseph's Egyptian owner tried to seduce Joseph, he ran from her with uncompromising principles. Is that the kind of attitude you have when faced with temptation? Or are you running toward temptation and sin full steam ahead? For those looking for

God's favor and relief from slavery, how is your purity? Does it match up to that of Joseph and his respect for marriage, regardless of your rough circumstances?

Debt and divorce are rampant in this age because sin is rampant, so take a long and sober look at your own life. People who fall into debt often get deeper into debt because they are unwilling to make the hard choices that take discipline and self-control to maintain. God does not bless such an irresponsible lifestyle. By contrast, Joseph, whose situation got worse when falsely accused and imprisoned, was a man who still honored God. Genesis 39:20-23 shows this; **"...But while Joseph was there in the prison, the LORD was with him; he showed him kindness and granted him favor in the eyes of the prison warden. So the warden put Joseph in charge of all those held in the prison, and he was made responsible for all that was done there. The warden paid no attention to anything under Joseph's care, because the LORD was with Joseph and gave him success in whatever he did."**

It is these sorts of people that God delights in: those who trust God even in difficult times and practice responsibility. Again, does this define you? Before wishfully jumping to say "yes," look at the facts of your life. Consider Joseph. Even in prison God approved of Joseph and allowed him to rise up and eventually lead the entire prison. Joseph did not walk around with an idle "woe is me" attitude. He took action--he ran the prison and brought order to chaos. Can the same be said for your situation? Are you known as a responsible man or woman? Is whatever you are leading prospering, or is it sinking? Closely examined, debt can be a form of slavery. In this day and age, it is a topic that most people worry about all-too-frequently, yet never talk about due to shame. Nevertheless through perseverance, Joseph was so remarkably rescued from slavery that only great faith aligning with our great God could have brought about such freedom.

Start praying this prayer with faith: "Lord, be with me as you were with Joseph. Please grant me success in whatever I do. Let it be according to your will, and advance your good purposes. Amen!"

God's dream for Joseph--and for us--is that we embrace his dream and submit to it even at the expense of personal comfort. Then if or when debt comes, it would not destroy us; it would refine us and lead to greater things. For Joseph, this meant he was exalted to become the leader of his family and the governor of Egypt--second only to Pharaoh in all the land. While others were going about their own business without preparing for the future, Joseph was given the foresight to deliver many nations out of the hands of famine and starvation. This did not come from a greedy heart. It came from a calm heart using money shrewdly in preparation to help many people.

Consider this account from Genesis 41. **"Joseph collected all the food produced in those seven years of abundance in Egypt and stored it in the cities. In each city he put the food grown in the fields surrounding it. Joseph stored up huge quantities of grain, like the sand of the sea; it was so much that he stopped keeping records because it was beyond measure.... When all Egypt began to feel the famine, the people cried to Pharaoh for food. Then Pharaoh told all the Egyptians, 'Go to Joseph and do what he tells you.' When the famine had spread over the whole country, Joseph opened the storehouses and sold grain to the Egyptians, for the famine was severe throughout Egypt. And all the countries came to Egypt to buy grain**

from Joseph, because the famine was severe in all the world." (Genesis 41:48-49 and Genesis 41:55-57)

Despite seemingly hopeless debt in his prior years, Joseph's purity and trust in God led to God's deepest approval and remarkable deliverance for many peoples. Notice how patient Joseph was about his plan. How could he be so patient? He trusted God, making sure his actions aligned with the will of God, in good times and bad.

In your own debt, if you also seek God's approval, then like Joseph, your purity, faith, and perseverance will be an example to imitate for generations to come. Your efforts will bring about God's rescue plan for many people. In this day and age, that means helping other people not be slaves to money, but become followers of Jesus Christ. That is what ultimately saves people (Matthew 28:19-20). There lies the hard road to becoming debt-free. Seek first God's kingdom and his righteousness (Matthew 6:33), because that is God's dream for us all. Like Joseph, dare to live God's dream. Dare to trust God despite the troubles. Dare to be a debt-buster.

The Future of Money

Inflation, disruptive technology, accidents, and our built-in aging process make for a rapidly and constantly changing world that looks very little like the world of olden days. Because our society is in constant transition, there will always be a temptation to worry about the unknown, and how we will make ends meet in an uncertain future. What we must do is adapt, grow, and re-position ourselves to face this unknown future with a persevering spirit. Pray that God gives us all the insight we need to be ready for whatever comes.

People, myself included, can get all worked up and even excited about a key element that will be a huge component of our immediate future: money. Yet what is money, really? Will there be money in heaven? I deeply doubt it. The Bible is very clear about what will survive the end of the world: nothing.

"But the day of the Lord will come like a thief. The heavens will disappear with a roar; the elements will be destroyed by fire, and the earth and everything in it will be laid bare. Since everything will be destroyed in this way, what kind of people ought you to be? You ought to live holy and godly lives as you look forward to the day of God and speed its coming. That day will bring about the destruction of the heavens by fire, and the elements will melt in the heat. But in keeping with his promise we are looking forward to a new heaven and a new earth, the home of righteousness." - 2 Peter 3:10-13

The passage starts with the definitive destruction of everything: **"the earth and everything in it will be laid bare."** The phrase translated "laid bare" is actually the Greek word "katakaio." That means to burn up, consume completely. Think about your bank account. Say you go to your bank one day and ask how much money is in your account. The bank teller replies, "Sorry, but your account has been laid bare." That means your bank account has absolutely nothing left in it. The money has been consumed wholly.

This passage also re-emphasizes the burning destiny of all things: **"the elements will melt in the heat."**

Retaining these verses from 2 Peter 3, now think about all the money in the entire world. Imagine the immense value of all the riches still in existence. On one hand, such wealth can be mind-boggling and even exciting: cash, coins, gold, diamonds, stocks, digital currency on flashy user friendly apps, digital tokens based on digital currency, and the list goes on. Just the thought of it can be very alluring. But on the other hand--the spiritual hand--everything, including all these forms of money, will all be "laid bare," as in nothing left. There is no wiggle room to set aside anything of material value, even a few little things, however portable they might appear to be. It is all destined for burning to the point where there will be nothing left at all. That is the real future of money--even the collective fumes and stench of its fiery end will not endure. For grand old money, that is the end of the story. Our spirit will live on to face God (Ecclesiastes 12:7), but money dies and stays dead.

In view of this sobering biblical certainty, we must re-evaluate how much we have elevated money and riches in our own lives, and especially in our hearts. Shame on us for not keeping God's clear end-game at the forefront of our thoughts and priorities. When you add up all the things God specifically says about the future, they all harmonize completely with an inescapable truth: money will not be the master of the followers of God. The followers, or anyone else, will not be taking money with them. The challenge for God's followers is to live like that now!

Before this world does end, there is another concept to wrap our heads around. How many years are we away from a scenario where paper money here on earth is frowned upon and even rejected as currency? This brings us to think about the fate of money on a near-future level. Technology has drastically changed the way we use money. It is already being recorded digitally with banks and credit card companies as simple data. In so many cases, no actual object really changes hands. You are really just transferring data (that has a perceived value) from one entity to the next.

Take this a step further. Will all the paper money and coins we currently use still be in place as real currency in ten years? We do not know. Certainly at the height of the Roman Empire, no one ever thought that its mighty coins would go out of circulation. But that is exactly what has happened to every currency since the earliest origins of money. Governments rise and fall, and with them so goes their money. Their currency, as physical objects, and its value, is gone. Truly, you cannot take it with you.

The Future of Money Is Here Now?

There could come a time when early adopters of something called cryptocurrency actually prefer to receive money exclusively in digital currency that is not bound to any government. Put very simply, cryptocurrency is digital money that is specially coded so that, theoretically, no one can steal it from the owner (unless they acquire the very long codes). For now, the most popular form of that cryptocurrency is bitcoin.

What is bitcoin? Since 2009, it has proliferated as a specific kind of encrypted digital currency that is already being used on a global scale. There are other forms of cryptocurrency beside bitcoin. Ether, which powers the ethereum network, is also a rising currency to watch, but bitcoin is by far the biggest alternative currency to date. Reading up on these disruptive technologies is like peering into the future from the present. It is somewhat stunning to think that these cryptocurrency transactions are going on right now and have been for years. It is as if the future is here now.

Where did cryptocurrencies like bitcoin come from? The idea started in science fiction stories decades ago. Once the Internet became real, many people around the globe wanted to make digital money that was not tied to any one country--it was for everyone and therefore decentralized. Think of bitcoin and ethereum as the real money of a virtual "country" called the Internet.

Bitcoin users are usually highly proactive about how to help newcomers cross over to wider bitcoin usage. They love to make new converts. They are very evangelistic; similar to real biblical evangelists, bitcoin enthusiasts are some of the most passionate, vocal, and innovative people when it comes to their spreading of the "good news" of bitcoin. More and more, bitcoin users are only too happy to teach others how to understand and use bitcoin. It has been going on for a few years already. Like the rest of the rapidly expanding user base of cryptocurrency, this is a massive global movement--the bitcoin movement.

At this point you might be getting excited, as in, how can I get me some bitcoins? Yet this is exactly where we need to put the brakes on, or at least press the "pause" button. No form of money should ever be a cause to live for. **"The love of money is the root of all kinds of evil"** (1 Timothy 6:10), so be warned. People must live for things eternal, and helping others along the way. It took me quite a long time from first hearing about bitcoin to actually investigating it as a useful form of currency. With all the other priorities I am committed to, I have to make sure personally that I am not living to serve bitcoin. I say this because, in a worldly sense, the bitcoin story is entirely fascinating, and sounds like science fiction, yet it is entirely true and operational right now. Nevertheless, I believe what Jesus says; **"You cannot serve both God and money"** (Matthew 6:24).

That said, as a Christian, a publisher, and a cartoonist, I am quite hopeful to see the mediums in which decentralized cryptocurrencies like bitcoin and ethereum might advance and prosper for all parties involved. If these technological innovations make it easier for missionaries to receive funds internationally, then so be it. I remember when webcomics (which is just a fancy term for online comics) were a new concept and people were trying to figure out an easy way to send micropayments (like little tips) to creators for posting these comics on the Internet. That never really got off the ground. But today, bitcoin and online comics could make a great combo for an online tipping platform. It might be fun to see what the future holds, as long as people do not make bitcoin their new god.

Before jumping on the bitcoin bandwagon, there is a lot more information to weigh out. Most investments (including buying bitcoin) are really calculated risks. Let me emphasize the word "risk." It is not much different than gambling, which is mostly about odds, chances, and even gut level feelings. But a calculated risk--an investment--in something such as bitcoin is best done after a person reviews enough information to make an educated decision that the level of risk, or gamble, is acceptable. In other words, that means you must be resolved for the possibility that your investment (risk, gamble) may fail. Make sure, if you invest in anything, that you are prepared to lose everything you put into that investment yet still be able to give to God and pay your bills because you only invested income that you could afford to lose. This is the key to investing (gambling) if you are inclined to do so in the first place.

It might surprise many to know that people who hold bitcoin right now do get a real value for it. This is not a case of "maybe this will be worth something some day." Bitcoin is worth something right now. In fact, the current market capitalization of bitcoin is over $10 billion US dollars and climbing. You can use it to buy all sorts of things instantly at this very moment online.

As for the future, only God knows what will really endure, whether it be bitcoin, the US dollar, or some other currency. Based on all the information I have absorbed, I believe both bitcoin and the US dollar have a lot of support and a lot of people/organizations fighting for each currency's ongoing establishment, expansion, and domination. But the scariest part about the future of money is the reason that these currencies are prospering: it is because people love money more than God.

So before anyone jumps into any investment, whether it be bitcoin, ethereum, stocks, or anything else, first go back to reviewing the biblical principles behind money. Are you giving generously to God and others? Are you now out of debt? Do you have a job that keeps the budget balanced? Have you tackled the greed in your life? Do you understand that it will all burn in the end? If the answer is "yes" to all of these questions, then maybe, and I do mean maybe, it might be wise--at some point--to invest in the stock market, real estate, cryptocurrency, or anything else that might be profitable. But remember what the Bible says about the pursuit of money; wealth **"is so uncertain"** (1 Timothy 6:17)! Do not even think about putting your hope in any investment. If you are investing in anything outside of God's kingdom, make sure you understand that this is a gamble and be prepared to lose it all.

One of the most unnerving financial points that cannot be stated enough regarding the future of money has to do with the conditional nature of any given currency; it could fall into a calamity beyond our control. Lamentations 3:38 shows the sovereignty of God. **"Is it not from the mouth of the Most High that both calamities and good things come?"** God, in his unsearchable wisdom and power, may decide it is time for one nation or another to enter into a period of calamity, as in disaster, distress, damage. Because we operate now in a global economy, when one nation suffers, the others are impacted as well. Therefore the whole world can change in an instant and feel the ripple effect of a slumping economy.

We could work so hard to save up and be "rich" in our holdings of a certain form of currency. We could be so responsible with our finances. Maybe it's the US dollar, bitcoin, euro, gold, ether, etc. But at any given moment, the specific system supporting any particular currency could be under attack or fall into decline, thus wiping away our riches. Indeed, wealth is so uncertain, which is why we must hope in God, not currency.

Yet as of this writing, many currencies sail full steam ahead. What is highly remarkable to me about today's popular currencies is how quickly the US Dollar and bitcoin have spread over the whole world and have become influencers of people in pretty much every nation on the planet. In a sense, these currencies have "evangelized the world." In the case of bitcoin, that global expansion to all nations has happened in less than a decade. Therefore, because of this spreading to all parts of the world, I imagine that there will be a significant place for both bitcoin and the US dollar for many years to come.

In the same way that evangelists of bitcoin and the US dollar use every opportunity to make their respective currency known to more and more people, my true hope and desire is for the proliferation of the eternal good news. As much as we would like to think otherwise, we cannot take our money with us to the grave. My prayer is that faithful followers will earn and be given all kinds of currency to finance biblical world evangelism: spreading the gospel of Jesus Christ to every corner of the world so that all nations will know that the only true path to God is through Jesus. Accept no counterfeits. As it is written in the Bible, Jesus is the only way to the Father (John 14:6), and there is no other name given by which we must be saved (Acts 4:12). Let everyone affirm with certainty, with no apology; "My hope is in Christ and his word."

The word of God is the only "currency" that reaches beyond the grave. Invest in that!

Convicted by the Widow's Offering

You won't find the following passage in many books about how to get out of debt. But we really must deal with this scripture because Jesus' observation about a certain widow's offering is one of the most convicting accounts about God and money in the entire Bible.

"As he looked up, Jesus saw the rich putting their gifts into the temple treasury. He also saw a poor widow put in two very small copper coins. 'I tell you the truth,' he said, 'this poor widow has put in more than all the others. All these people gave their gifts out of their wealth; but she out of her poverty put in all she had to live on.'" - Luke 21:1-4

How should a person wanting to get out of debt respond to the radical trust of this amazing widow and her massive offering to God? It seems counterintuitive to all practical financial wisdom. Do we need to obey this example of radical giving? Should we just dismiss all other financial advice to simply give all our money to God in one lump sum, forfeiting all hope of ever becoming debt-free?

I think not; you do not have to do that. What the widow did is not a command, and she must have done it in hope that God would answer some vital need of hers. Yet just because this account did not come with a command, that doesn't mean we can dismiss the lessons layered into what happened. After all, this widow's offering made it into the Bible, not just in Luke, but also the parallel account in Mark 12:41-44. So we must learn much from her act of faith.

While the widow's actions are convicting to even the most committed Christians today, the passage is not isolated. It still needs to harmonize with the rest of the scriptures, not the least of which is the verse in Romans 13:8 about letting **"no debt remain outstanding."** In other words, if people in debt liquidated everything they had and then gave it to the church, then their debts would really be even more outstanding, with no plan to pay off each member's creditor. Those in debt, therefore, retain their personal responsibility to pay off their debt.

Nevertheless, there is still so much to challenge us about the widow's offering. The heart behind the widow's offering is that she totally trusted God with her future. Can we say the same?

Before saying that we do trust God with our future, consider that the widow put her immediate future in God's hands. She gave **"all she had to live on."** Can we really say that we trust God with our immediate future? What faithful action are you taking to show such a commitment? The widow left no doubt where she put all her trust. She trusted in God; she bet it all on him, with no back up plan. That is extreme faith--the kind that pleases God.

I can't help but be more than a little curious about what happened to her the following day. She was poor. She was a widow, and now she had no money at all. Yet she had one huge thing in her favor; she had the certain attention of the Son of God, and his personal commendation.

Combining such things with the rest of the scriptures, in faith, we must understand that God somehow took care of her. We don't know what exactly this looked like. We don't know if it was the following hour, the next day, or if she had to wait a while, but we must believe that God provided a way for her future needs to get met.

Scriptures like Psalm 37:28 must apply here. **"For the LORD loves the just and will not forsake his faithful ones. They will be protected forever...."** Whether God helped the widow find a new job, or her next payday was known to be the following day, or a far-off relative came through with sudden money, or some other surprise benefits, the remarkable and convicting thing about this widow is that she put it all on the line for God.

She must have had some of the most extreme trust in God ever recorded in history. That should take away all of our excuses. In fact, any excuse I could imagine to justify why I would not do what the widow had done just sounds trivial, wimpy, and selfish. I think that's the point. God is saying to me "Do you think you are faithful? Really? Well take a look at this widow's example of faith? Do you still think you are so faithful?"

Through his word, Jesus calls us higher in our faith and our giving through the widow's example of trust and selflessness. Therefore whatever we do with our money, make sure trusting God with extreme faith is a key component of our spending and earning patterns.

Should I be so bold as to direct you to take everything you have to live on and give it to the church? No. That's not what happened with this widow. Jesus did not tell her to do this. It was her own decision. If you decide to do such a thing, it must be your own decision, and it must also harmonize with the rest of the scriptures.

Whatever you do with your money, keep going back, from time to time, to the example of the widow's offering. It's in the Bible for many reasons and there are a lifetime of lessons to learn from this woman. If we are paying attention, then the widow's offering will humble us every time. This is where God wants us: having a reverence and a trust in him, not money.

Epilogue: The Parable of the Secret War

The following is a simplistic parable designed to help increase your awareness of the battle going on right now for your money, your life, and your very soul.

Once upon a time, in a world gone mad, there was a secret war. Only a few brave people fought directly on the good side of this conflict. These folks fought in such a way that it pleased their master. Their attitudes and actions were honorable and delightful. Consequently, the master favored them, and even fought with them against the enemy.

The rest of the people stayed home, fell in love with money, got into terrible debt and watched a lot of TV and streaming videos on their expensive smartphones. These people thought that they were not at all in any battle; they thought they were safe on the sidelines--yet they were deceived. Their love for money strengthened the position of an unseen evil one--

fuelling his deadly weapons of destruction. As more people became lazy and fell deeper in love with money, the evil one grew more and more powerful.

Yet the faithful never gave up. After many battles had ebbed and flowed, the fighters on the good side of the war were finally transferred to a wonderful realm beyond description. They were not the best fighters, yet they gave their very best. Therefore victory was handed to them because they pleased the master, who fought most vigilantly for their benefit and advancement.

These noble fighters received the greatest reward: to dwell with the master of the mightiest kingdom that will ever be. They were whisked away by the master to the farthest horizon, to a paradise long forgotten. And those few merry soldiers lived happily ever after--amongst new riches beyond imagination.

About the Author

Renaissance man might be the best way to describe Joe Chiappetta. He is an Author, Cartoonist, Painter, Photographer, Christian Ministry Leader, Publisher, Community Organizer, Program Director, Researcher, Choir Singer, and Trainer.

As the author of over a dozen nonfiction and fiction books, as well as numerous magazines and articles, Chiappetta has won many awards. This includes an Illinois Arts Council Award for his work on the project: "Back Pain Avenger/Disability in Comics." The book, research, and speaking tour surrounding the Award focused on issues of disability in the history of comic books, as well as presenting a non-medicated memoir of rehabilitation.

For his family documentary and experimental work on the graphic novel "Silly Daddy," Joe was the recipient of the Xeric Award as well as numerous other award nominations over the years. Silly Daddy is also the ongoing title of his comic strip series, one of the longest running autobiographical comics in the world. Chiappetta is a husband and father of three who loves God and bicycle riding.

In 1999, Joe began leading community Bible discussion groups in the Chicago area, and most recently in Pasadena, California. He's one of the founding members of the Chicago International Christian Church, is a current leader in the City of Angeles International Christian Church and leads both members and non-members in areas of applied Christianity, parenting, marriage, service to the poor and those with disabilities, as well as mental health recovery matters.

Joe has served as the Director of MERCY*WORLDWIDE* for their Chicago Branch, and currently for their Los Angeles Branch. MERCY*WORLDWIDE* is a global nonprofit charity. Chiappetta increased the scope of this organization from annual to monthly service projects helping people with disabilities as well as those who are poor.

Joe is also the founder of Chicago's Workforce Developer Network (WDN). It's the oldest collaborative of organizations working together to place more people with disabilities in jobs. In 2014, the group had a record-setting year; employers hired 137 people with disabilities through WDN, which generated nearly $2 million in benefits to society.

For the thousands of people who have become employed with the help of this collaborative, Joe was included as part of a

Chicago delegation to Washington DC that was awarded the US Department of Labor's New Freedom Initiative Award. This took place while Joe was Director of Workforce Development at the Chicagoland Chamber of Commerce. He has also served as group leader on Chicago's Mayoral Task Force on the Employment of People with Disabilities.

As Director and Coordinator of Employment Services for a number of nonprofit agencies over the years, Joe built a strong reputation of revitalizing staff to eliminate program waste and place more people with disabilities in jobs. He has helped agencies expand their innovation and marketing agendas to improve placement results.

Chiappetta has been an interdisciplinary researcher and research advisory team member in many major projects on disability studies, employment matters, religion, and comics history. Research has been conducted for, or in partnership with, a number of organizations, including DePaul University, Illinois Department of Commerce and Economic Opportunity, Chicagoland Chamber of Commerce, Illinois Arts Council, Chicago International Christian Church, Access Living, and MERCY*WORLDWIDE*.

Joe has been a trainer and curriculum designer on disability-employment matters to many employers, a variety of State and nonprofit agencies, universities, high schools, parent groups and persons with disabilities. This includes Chicago Public Schools, ComEd, Compass Group, Exelon, Illinois Division of Rehabilitation Services, KPMG, Manpower, National Louis University, PepsiCo, Sodexo, University of Illinois at Chicago, Walgreens, Walmart, and almost every job placement agency serving people with disabilities in the Chicago area.

Joe received a Bachelor of Arts in Ministry and Charity Services from the International College of Christian Ministries in Los Angeles. He's also an alumni of Northern Illinois University with a Bachelor of Fine Arts who graduated cum laude and received the Dean's Award. His interdisciplinary education and experiences have encouraged him to use creativity combined with integrity to live a meaningful life to the full.

Catalog: View Published Works by Chiappetta

For a complete list of available books published by Chiappetta, including ordering information, go to **http://joechiappetta.blogspot.com/p/books.html**.

NONFICTION

Mighty Messianic Prophecy: Biblical Research of Predictions Proving that Jesus Is God (paperback and eBook)

Find Jesus in the Old Testament right now! Discover how the story of Jesus has been thinly yet astonishingly veiled in the Old Testament and just waiting for you to gain a rich appreciation into the very nature of God. In this book of biblical research designed to unlock the deeper truths of Christianity, see how analysis of Scripture can propel your faith and understanding to new heights. This massive Christian study guide is a non-fiction, no-nonsense, non-stop examination of the predictions proving Jesus to be the definitive and only Lord for all people and all nations.

The Back Pain Avenger: Heal Chronic Back Pain and Destroy It Forever (paperback and eBook)

A non-medicated memoir of rehabilitation. Discover how one eccentric leader in the disability community finally overcomes his own back injury and no longer suffers from chronic back pain. Find out if the unorthodox methods he uses in healing back pain will work for you. Disability advocates, people with disabilities, their family members, as well as healthcare professionals and businesses who employ people with disabilities will be aching with laughs, insight, and the awareness that brings healing in this lighthearted yet powerful journey. Alternative medicine meets cartoon humor and the Bible. The book also includes Disability in Comics: a chronological index of major characters with disabilities featured in the history of comic books and strips.

Silly Daddy 2004 graphic novel (paperback)

Imagine Van Gogh with a wife and kid today: that's Silly Daddy. Parenting has rarely been more profound. A Xeric award winning cartoonist turns autobiographical storytelling into a family odyssey of road trips, break-ups, romance, sci-fi adventure, big laughs, deep thoughts, family bonding, and redemption.

Crucified Comics (eBook)

Go beyond a cartoon view of the cross with comics and spiritual commentary aimed to inspire personal accountability for what happened to Jesus at the crucifixion. If you sense that this Christian book preaches, you're right. Buckle up for some faithful devotionals. Those curious about seeking God as well as long-time church members will find much to deepen their beliefs about having a daily walk with the Lord. This mix of comic book and text narrative has plenty of practical lessons for your reading and prayer times with God.

Mega Debt-Busters: A Christian Guide to Financial Freedom (paperback and eBook)

Get out of debt by applying powerful biblical truths. Prepare your mind and your wallet for useful financial action that honors God. Learn how to approach God and money as defined by Jesus, the author of life. If you are in financial debt or just want help managing money from a spiritual perspective, this is for you. Tackle hidden greed, inefficiency, and even unidentified laziness in your life that will lead you to a balanced budget and a greater faith. With God, patience, faith and discipline, you can bust out from under the shackles of your creditors and become debt-free.

Rescuing Supermom: Essays and Poetry to Enrich a Mother's Soul (eBook)

Chick lit with true grit by Denise Chiappetta. Erma Bombeck meets Mary Magdalene and the result might be this book. Motherhood, sisterhood, womanhood and wife-hood come under the crosshairs of an author who strives to be her best for God and family.

FICTION

Star Chosen: a science fiction novel (paperback and eBook)

Think "Star Trek" meets the Bible. Deleting history was just the beginning. Blast off with this space opera of post-biblical proportions! After war, heartbreak, attacks to your faith, and the erasure of all history, whose side will you fight on: the Proud... or the Chosen?

Power Pendant of Planet Pizon: a Star Chosen sci-fi novelette (eBook)

The Star Chosen are caught in a deadly struggle over a mysterious power pendant that may be the only thing standing between them and certain vaporization. When control over this otherworldly pendant gets called into controversy, a young romance on Planet Pizon turns into a fatal battle involving laser guns, spaceships, and ex-boyfriends.

Armed with Intergalactic Weapons (sci-fi illustrated eBook)

Autobiographical short story of Joe Chiappetta's Christian conversion story retold as if he lived in the far off future. See how a space boy becomes a sci-fi fighter and an artist--on the wrong and right sides in the galactic battle between good and evil.

Silly Daddy in Space comic book (eBook)

Take a lighthearted yet insightful view of the future with science fiction, robots, aliens, and futuristic gadgets. Ideal for geek dads, geek moms, nerds, aspiring nerds, and anyone looking for good, clean, deep-space laughs. It's sci-fi satire safe for all ages and androids too! Inside jokes and parodies abound for fans of Star Wars, Battlestar Galactica, and Star Trek. The colorful cast of offworld characters includes Office Space Girl, Christian Robot, funny and weird aliens, plus the whole Silly Daddy family.

Genesis Jam: An Anthology Inspired by the Ultimate Creator (eBook)

Creative writers and artists striving to love God embrace the powerful themes of Genesis: good and evil, brotherhood, family, trust in God, mercy, and love. The Garden of Eden and Cain and Abel are the subjects of this faithful anthology. Works of fiction inspired by events in Genesis as well as nonfiction pieces about the first family are covered.

www.ingramcontent.com/pod-product-compliance
Lightning Source LLC
Chambersburg PA
CBHW060358190526
45169CB00002B/651